The MIRACLES of JESUS

BIBLE WISDOM FOR TODAY

The MIRACLES of JESUS

JAMES HARPUR

REV. MARCUS BRAYBROOKE
CONSULTANT

The Reader's Digest Association, Inc.
Pleasantville, New York • Montreal

A Reader's Digest Book
Conceived, edited, and designed by
Marshall Editions
170 Piccadilly, London W1V 9DD

Project editor: James Bremner
Art editor: Helen Spencer
Picture editor: Elizabeth Loving
Research: Michaela Moher
DTP editors: Mary Pickles, Kate Waghorn
Copy editor: Jolika Feszt
Managing editor: Lindsay McTeague
Production editor: Emma Dixon
Production: Robert K. Christie
Art director: Sean Keogh
Editorial director: Sophie Collins

The publishers acknowledge Rev. Marcus Braybrooke as author
of the Introduction and the "Messages for Today."

The acknowledgments that appear on page 96 are hereby made a
part of this copyright page.

First North American Edition

Library of Congress Cataloging in Publication Data

Harpur, James.
    The miracles of Jesus / James Harpur : Marcus Braybrooke,
consultant. — 1st North American ed.
        p.   cm. — (Bible wisdom for today : v. 1)
    Includes bibliographical references and index.
    ISBN 0-89577-907-2
    1. Jesus Christ — Miracles. I. Braybrooke, Marcus. II. Title.
III. Series.
    BT366.H39   1997
232.9'55—dc20   96-29132
                                             CIP

Origination by HBM Print, Singapore
Printed and bound in Italy by Chromolitho

Pictures shown on the preliminary pages are:
(page one) Jesus, walking on water and saving Peter from drowning
in the Sea of Galilee, in a detail from a 19th-century British
stained-glass window; (page two) the Western Wall in Jerusalem;
(page three) the Sea of Galilee; (page five) Christ's Miracles of
Healing, from the 13th-century French Bible Moralisée.

CONTENTS

*This fifth-century Roman ivory panel shows some of Jesus' miracles,
including: the raising of Lazarus (top, right); healing the blind man and the
wedding at Cana (middle); and curing the paralytic and the leper (bottom).*

INTRODUCTION

"What really happened?" is the question many modern readers ask about the miracles that Jesus is said to have performed during his ministry in Palestine about 2,000 years ago. But the Gospel writers – by tradition the evangelists Matthew, Mark, Luke, and John – who recorded the events pose a different question: "What do you think about the person who performed the miracles?" John, for example, says that he recorded them so that the reader might "believe that Jesus is the Christ, the Son of God [20:31]."

In the late 20th century, many people, particularly in the Western world, find it difficult to believe wholeheartedly in miracles. Some may assume that science can, in principle, explain all phenomena and that seemingly inexplicable events will eventually be accounted for. Those who share this view would probably suggest that Jesus' contemporaries, living in an unscientific age, regarded as miraculous occurrences that could now be given a rational explanation.

✝ *Healing and nature miracles* ✝

Biblical scholars have often made the distinction between Jesus' healing miracles and his "nature" miracles – those involving the natural world, such as the quieting of a storm. Many people find it easier to accept some of Jesus' cures in the light of findings about the psychosomatic nature of some illnesses. But nature miracles demand a greater stretch of faith and have attracted a wide range of rational responses.

Because the only record of the miracles is in the Gospels, which were written in the second half of the first century AD – a generation, at least, after the death of Jesus – any explanations of them tend to be speculative. In fact, the Gospels were not intended as histories or biographies: their primary purpose was to encourage faith in Jesus Christ. Before the first Gospel texts appeared, the miracle stories were used by the early Christians in their sermons and may have been adapted to suit specific circumstances. In this way, the accounts reflect to some extent the concerns of the early church, for example, the growing bitterness between the Jewish and Christian communities.

Although the first three Gospels – those of Matthew, Mark, and Luke – are usually called "Synoptic" because they describe the life of

The symbols used in the panels on top of each page represent the four Gospel writers. The lion symbolizes Mark; the man, Matthew; the ox, Luke; and the eagle, John. The symbols show the Gospel sources for each story.

Jesus from a similar point of view, each has its own emphasis. Mark saw the miracles, particularly the exorcisms, as evidence that the power of God was present in Jesus' ministry to defeat evil and usher in God's kingdom. Matthew wrote primarily for Jewish, not Gentile, Christians. Luke aimed his gospel chiefly at the Gentiles and stressed Jesus' compassion for the troubled and vulnerable. John's Gospel was written later than the other three and differs from them in content and organization. John speaks of the miracles as signs that made known who Jesus really was – they "revealed his glory" (2:11).

In fact, all the evangelists saw the miracles as evidence of Jesus' divine nature and were careful to avoid giving the impression that Jesus was just another of the itinerant "wonder-workers" who existed at that time. And Jesus' opponents did not debate so much that he had performed a miracle as by what authority he had performed it.

† A God who intervenes? †

The debate about Jesus' miracles is as vigorous today as it was at the time of his ministry. Different attitudes toward them reflect contrasting personal world views. Atheistic materialists, for example, will view them differently from those who believe the world is a sphere of divine activity. Even Christians are divided. Those who believe that miracles are refuted by modern science may view them symbolically rather than literally. Some may be concerned about the idea of an interventionist God. Why, they may ask, if some people are "miraculously" cured, does God allow others to suffer excruciating pain? Some may also wish to stress the full humanity of Jesus and question whether he exercised supernatural powers. Still others, who interpret the miracles literally, may also hold that God's power to heal may be revealed in a person's attitude to illness rather than through a physical cure.

In this book, the miracles as recorded in the Gospels – from the wedding at Cana to the miraculous haul of fish after Jesus' Resurrection – are retold, set in context, and discussed. The sequence is based as far as possible on the chronology of the Gospels, but the indications of time and place are often imprecise. It is thought that Jesus, who was born in about 6 BC – not AD 1 as was once believed – was in his thirties when he began his ministry in Galilee, Judea, and other parts of Palestine.

Those who, long ago, witnessed the miracles asked themselves about the authority of Jesus. Today, any discussion of the miracles raises the same question. Yet even those who do not share the church's traditional belief that Jesus is the Son of God, or who doubt whether the miracles actually happened, may find a relevant message for today in the way Jesus cared for those in need and met the criticisms of his opponents.

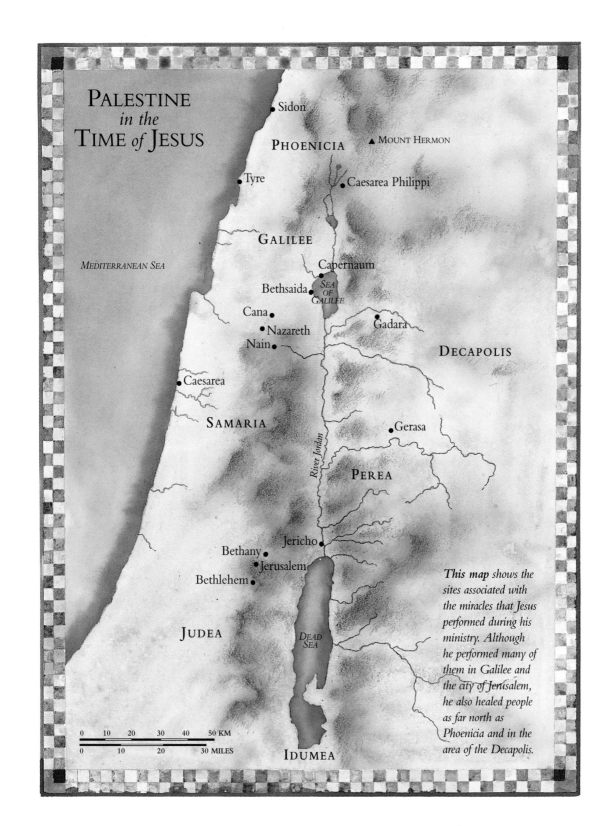

PALESTINE
in the
TIME *of* JESUS

Sidon

PHOENICIA

▲ MOUNT HERMON

Tyre

Caesarea Philippi

GALILEE

MEDITERRANEAN SEA

Capernaum

Bethsaida

SEA OF GALILEE

Cana

Nazareth

Gadara

Nain

DECAPOLIS

Caesarea

SAMARIA

Gerasa

River Jordan

PEREA

Jericho

Bethany

Jerusalem

Bethlehem

JUDEA

DEAD SEA

This map shows the
sites associated with
the miracles that Jesus
performed during his
ministry. Although
he performed many of
them in Galilee and
the city of Jerusalem,
he also healed people
as far north as
Phoenicia and in the
area of the Decapolis.

| 0 | 10 | 20 | 30 | 40 | 50 KM |
| 0 | 10 | 20 | 30 MILES |

IDUMEA

The WINE of TRANSFORMATION

The WEDDING at CANA

JOHN 2:1–11

*" On the third day there was a wedding at Cana in Galilee...
And they ran out of wine, since the wine provided
for the feast had all been used, and the mother of Jesus said
to him, 'They have no wine.' "*

JOHN 2:1–3

THE MIRACLES that Jesus performed played a central part in his ministry to the people of ancient Palestine and, according to the Gospels, were manifestations of his status as the Son of God. In John's Gospel, the first of Jesus' miracles took place in the town of Cana, traditionally thought to be the modern Kafar Kanna, situated north of Nazareth in Galilee. The scene was a wedding feast. John does not state who the bride and bridegroom were, but it is likely they were good friends of Jesus because his mother, Mary, and his disciples had also been invited to the celebration.

During the feast, Mary noticed that the wine had run out and alerted Jesus. Her son's reply – "Woman, what do you want from me?" – seems stern. However, "woman" was a customary form of address, and Jesus was also using a standard phrase of the times, telling Mary not to interfere and to reassure her that he was in control of the situation. So Mary, sensing that further requests for Jesus' intervention would be fruitless, told the servants to do whatever Jesus told them to do.

By the side of the room stood six large empty stone jars – each with nearly 30 gallons (114 liters) capacity – reserved for ceremonial washing.

(According to Jewish convention, people's hands and tableware had to be washed before a meal for the sake of ritual purity.) Jesus ordered the servants to fill these vessels with water. He then told them to give some to the president of the feast, who might have been a toastmaster or an important guest who had been asked to organize the seating and other arrangements.

+ Water into wine +

The servants did what Jesus told them. But the water that the president tasted had miraculously turned to wine, and he, not knowing where it had come from, saluted the bridegroom with the words, "Everyone serves good wine first and the worse wine when the guests are well wined; but you have kept the best wine till now."

The Gospel account then ends abruptly with the words: "This was the first of Jesus' signs…He revealed his glory, and his disciples believed in him. After this he went down to Capernaum with his mother and his brothers and his disciples, but they stayed there only a few days."

Modern scholars draw a distinction between miracles of healing and those that involved the

natural world, such as when Jesus walked on water or fed thousands of people with a few fish and bread loaves. This miracle is, according to John, the first of the "nature" miracles told in the Gospels. He stresses how the miracle demonstrated both Jesus' divinity and his humanity.

Jewish weddings were festive occasions. The bridegroom and bride were dressed up, treated, and addressed as a king and queen, and the feasting, drinking, music, and dancing often lasted as long as a week. Jesus is sometimes portrayed as a solitary ascetic; but his presence at the wedding showed that he valued the traditional rituals of society and approved of the merrymaking. Clearly, he did not think it was wrong to enjoy

Mary, shown at left with a halo, turns to Jesus to tell him that the wine has run out, in this medieval Serbian fresco. At right, a servant fills large storage jars with water that Jesus changed into wine.

the pleasures of food and drink, unlike the self-denying John the Baptist; John lived on locusts and wild honey while preaching to ready his listeners for Jesus' ministry. In contrast, at this wedding, Jesus was even prepared to work a miracle that prolonged the festive atmosphere.

The transformation of water into wine, which appears to be so contrary to the scientific outlook of the modern Western world, has caused much debate among biblical scholars, some of whom have sought to explain it along rationalist lines. One such interpretation is that the vessels were already half full of wine and that the charismatic presence of Jesus was such that the guests tasted the diluted drink as a top vintage.

> ❝ *Jesus said to the servants, 'Fill the jars with water,' and they filled them to the brim.* ❞
>
> JOHN 2:7

Other commentators, however, believe that there is no need to question the ability of Jesus to perform the miracle, working as he was with the power of God, the Creator of nature. As the British author C. S. Lewis wrote: "Every year, as part of the natural order, God makes wine. He does so by creating a vegetable organism that can turn water, soil and sunlight into a juice which will, under proper conditions, become wine… Once, and in one year only, God, now incarnate, short-circuits the process; makes wine in a moment; uses earthenware jars instead of vegetable fibers to hold the water."

Through his account of the miracle, John hoped his readers would recognize the glory of God in action and put their faith in God. John might also have wanted them to notice the allusions and symbolic elements that the story contains. By tradition, John wrote his Gospel in the Greek city of Ephesus in Asia Minor, and for

Ancient Cana has been identified with modern Kafar Kanna, near Nazareth, in Israel. The traditional site of the wedding feast is now marked by a church.

Large amphorae such as these held up to 30 gallons (114 liters) and were used to store water, wine, and other liquids in most wealthy Jewish households.

his Greek readers, the miracle would have naturally recalled their god of wine, Dionysus, who was also credited with miraculously creating the drink.

That the miracle took place at a wedding feast may also symbolize a deeper spiritual truth. In the Gospels, Jesus is sometimes alluded to as "the bridegroom," and his followers – the Church – as his bride, just as in the Old Testament God was said to be the bridegroom of Israel. The true bridegroom came to the wedding feast of two representatives of the Jewish religion and performed a miracle, a sign of the new marriage between God (through Jesus) and his people.

John may also have intended the six stone vessels of water, used for Jewish purification rites, to represent Judaism. The water – that is the Law – then reached fulfillment only when Jesus transformed it into a superabundance of wine – the Gospel he was teaching. This miraculously created wine – which early Christian readers would have associated with the wine served at their service of the Eucharist, or Mass – represents the communion with God made possible by Jesus. And this relationship, Christians believe, is embodied in the holy sacrament of marriage. ✦

Message
—for—
Today

THE MIRACLE AT Cana features two symbolic elements – wine and marriage – that are as potent for Christians today as they were for the early followers of Christ. On more than one occasion, Jesus identified his own blood with wine, and insisted that only by drinking it could people experience its transforming power: "If you do not eat the flesh of the Son of man and drink his blood, you have no life in you (John 6:53)."

Further, his relationship with the faithful, he suggested, was as close as the union between a bridegroom and bride. So, for Christians, a wedding is not only a sacred ceremony by which husband and wife become "one flesh." It is in itself a living embodiment of the loving bond between Jesus and his Church.

DRIVING OUT *the* POWERS *of* DARKNESS

The POSSESSED MAN *at* CAPERNAUM

MARK 1:21–28; LUKE 4:36–37

> ❝ *They went as far as Capernaum, and at once on the Sabbath he went into the synagogue and began to teach. And his teaching made a deep impression on them because, unlike the scribes, he taught them with authority. And at once in their synagogue there was a man with an unclean spirit.* ❞
>
> MARK 1:21–23

CCORDING TO the Gospels, Jesus had the power to cure not only physical illness, but also spiritual affliction – the dreadful effects of evil spirits on those who were thought to be possessed. The first person with a spiritual affliction encountered by Jesus was in the town of Capernaum in the district of Galilee. Jesus had just come from the Sea of Galilee, so Mark's Gospel relates, where he had recruited the first four of his twelve disciples – Simon Peter, Andrew, James, and John. They arrived in Capernaum on the Sabbath, and Jesus decided to go to the local synagogue, where he immediately began to teach.

Mark records that Jesus caused quite a stir among the assembled worshipers. They were used to the teaching of the "scribes." These men – not really experts in writing or transliteration as their name suggests, but specialists in Jewish Law – used their encyclopedic knowledge of the Scriptures to instruct the common people. Jesus, however, instead of appealing to tradition, spoke to them with the direct authority of God.

While Jesus was still teaching inside the synagogue, a distressed voice among the audience suddenly rang out with the words: "What do you want with us, Jesus of Nazareth? Have you come to destroy us? I know who you are: the Holy One of God."

† Exorcizing the demon †

The voice belonged to a man with an "unclean spirit" – in other words, a man possessed by a demon. Jesus' response was instantaneous and masterful. With a peremptory command, he ordered the demon to be silent and leave the man. Immediately, the spirit threw the man into a fit of convulsions, then left his body with a loud cry.

The effect on the onlookers was dramatic. A general hubbub broke out and people asked each other what it could possibly mean that Jesus was able not only to speak for God but also to control evil spirits. His reputation, according to Mark, "at once spread everywhere, through all the surrounding Galilean countryside."

Belief in demons was widespread in the ancient world. "Demon" is derived from the Greek word *daimon*, and the Greeks originally looked upon *daimons* as minor gods or supernatural forces without the negative associations.

But in Judaism and Christianity – and, later, Islam – demons were looked upon as forces opposed to God and humankind. Unlike the angels, who inhabited the realm of light (God's kingdom), demons existed in the kingdom of darkness, with Satan as their king. According to the apocryphal Old Testament Book of Enoch,

Jesus exorcizes the demoniac in this medieval 11th-century German book illumination. As Jesus gestures to the possessed man, the evil spirit in the form of a miniature devil comes forth from his mouth.

demons were originally the sons of gods. In fact, early Christian scholars, such as the third-century theologian Origen, believed that demons were fallen angels. In any case, as the Gospels show, demons had the capacity to possess people and afflict them with various ailments and illnesses, such as leprosy and paralysis.

The third-century synagogue at Capernaum, shown here, was excavated in 1981. As a result, it was confirmed that the building stood on the remains of a first-century structure – possibly the one in which Jesus exorcized the demoniac.

According to the Gospel accounts, the demons seemed to know who Jesus was as soon as they entered his presence. Thus, in the Capernaum synagogue, the possessed man addressed Jesus as the "Holy One of God." This is one of the ironies of the Gospels – that while the evil spirits apparently had a supernatural insight into the spiritual nature of Jesus, the ordinary people and, to a lesser extent, Jesus' own disciples were not able to perceive his true divine status.

Of course, the demons might have had ulterior motives in declaring Jesus' name. It was a common belief in ancient times that a person's name had a power in itself, and that with knowledge of someone's name went the ability to exert control over him or her. So when the Capernaum demoniac cried out, "What do you want with us, Jesus of Nazareth?" he could have been trying to counter the power of Jesus.

✝ Satan's power ✝

The evil spirit's exorcism helped to spread the word about Jesus' divine power. But according to the Gospels, Jesus was not the only exorcist operating at this time. And on at least one later occasion, he was accused of driving devils out through the power of Beelzebul, the prince of the devils – that is, Satan. Jesus retorted that Satan would not weaken himself by granting the power to drive out his own devils. He then went on to say: "And if it is through Beelzebul that I drive devils out, through whom *do your own experts* [author's italics] drive them out? [Matthew 12:27]."

> ❝ *Astonishment seized them*
> *and they were all saying*
> *to one another, 'What is*
> *it in his words? He gives orders*
> *to unclean spirits with*
> *authority and power and*
> *they come out.'* ❞
>
> LUKE 4:36

The accusation made by his enemies shows that Jesus' exorcisms did not incontrovertibly prove his divine authority to them. His contemporaries may well have construed him to be someone well versed in the magic arts, as a Samaritan named Simon was later said to be (Acts 8). Apparently, they did not recognize the outward differences between Jesus and the other exorcists who were operating in the Greco-Roman world at that time. Many of them seem to have openly identified themselves with various deities, such as the Greek god Hermes or the Egyptian god Osiris, and used magical aids, such as perfumes, to help them perform their exorcisms.

Jesus did not try to impress people by publicly stating his relationship with God. Nor did he use complex magical rituals. He simply spoke; his command was sufficient to drive out the demons. Certainly, for the Gospel writers, Jesus' exorcisms, like his healings, were signs that the kingdom of God was being established on Earth, taking over the domain that had been formerly subject to the powers of evil. ✦

MESSAGE
—for—
TODAY

WHEN THE ASSEMBLED worshipers in the Capernaum synagogue saw Jesus for the first time, they were impressed by his teaching. Yet it was the possessed man who correctly perceived the nature of Jesus' authority, whose divine provenance Mark later emphasizes by saying that Jesus went off by himself to commune with God through prayer (1:35).

Jesus told the evil spirit to be silent, perhaps because he did not want people to believe in his divinity because they were afraid or astonished. Nor did he want them to misunderstand his mission.

Divine authority has its foundation based on the power of truth. So those who wish to share their faith with others have no need to be coercive. Nothing is more convincing than a faith lived out with integrity and love for others.

A PRIVATE CURE

PETER'S MOTHER-in-LAW

MARK 1:29–34; MATTHEW 8:14–17;
LUKE 4:38–41

❝ *He went in to her, took her by the hand and helped her up.* **❞**
MARK 1:31

AFTER HIS exorcism of the possessed man in the synagogue at Capernaum (pp. 14–17), Jesus went directly to the house of Simon Peter (later known as Peter) and his brother Andrew. They were accompanied, according to Mark, by James and John. Inside the house, Jesus was told that Peter's mother-in-law was ill. Mark says she was suffering from a fever, and Luke, who by tradition was a doctor, called it a "great" or "high" fever.

Jesus was taken in to see the patient and, in Mark's account, he went up to her without a word, took her by the hand, and raised her up. Luke states that Jesus "rebuked" the fever. In both accounts, the effect was immediate: the fever not only left her, but she was also able to "serve them."

The apostle Peter, at right, cranes forward to watch Jesus heal his mother-in-law, in this painting by the 19th-century British artist John Bridges.

Although the cure of Peter's mother-in-law lacks the drama of, say, the raising of Lazarus (pp. 70–73) and does not end with Jesus making a significant pronouncement about faith, prayer, or another aspect of Christian life, it does convey a sense of intimacy and authenticity. It provides an insight into the world of Jesus behind closed doors, away from the spotlight of his public ministry.

It also shows the level of Jesus' compassion. He must have been drained from his experience in the synagogue, yet he was willing to bring miraculous aid at the tacit request of a friend as surely as he would show his power in front of crowds. By implication, this miracle also demonstrates the bond that had already formed between Jesus and Peter, Andrew, James, and John, whom, according to Mark, he had only just called to be his disciples. And it shows the power of Jesus' healing that, after her cure, Peter's mother-in-law was immediately well enough to set about preparing and serving food for them.

† After sunset †

Some biographical insight can also be gleaned from the story. When Mark relates that Jesus had called Peter and Andrew to be his disciples, it is not stated whether they were single or married, only that they were fishermen. Now it can be inferred that Peter was a married man and dutiful toward his wife's mother.

Jesus stayed in Peter's house – which probably became the headquarters for his Galilean ministry – for the rest of the day. Then, after sunset, people began to arrive at the house, bringing with them "all who were sick and those who were possessed by devils." Sunset signaled the end of the Sabbath, the day when, according to Jewish Law, all work was suspended to commemorate the "seventh day" on which God rested after his creation of the universe (Exodus 20:8–11). So, as darkness settled over the city, large numbers of people made their way to Peter's house, and Jesus cured and exorcized many of them. ✦

MESSAGE
—for—
TODAY

JESUS WAS often surrounded by people pleading for his help. Even so, he was not too busy to set aside time for private prayer or to notice the troubles of those closest to him.

The pressures of modern life may blind people to the needs of others, even the problems of those with whom they live. Working "all hours" to provide a high standard of living, they may fail to give their partner or children the emotional support they need. Jesus brought divine resources to the needs of others. Built into the exercise of faith is the understanding that divine resources are available to all who believe. A growing number of people recognize the importance of making time for prayer, meditation, or retreats. Refreshed from these periods of quiet, they can return to the rigors of everyday life, better able to care for those who are close to them.

An ACT of CLEANSING

The MAN with the SKIN DISEASE

MARK 1:40–44; MATTHEW 8:1–4; LUKE 5:12–16

*❝ A man suffering from a virulent skin disease came to him...
saying, 'If you are willing, you can cleanse me.' ❞*

MARK 1:40

T HE MORNING after he had cured Peter's mother-in-law and other sick and possessed people, Jesus left Capernaum, Mark's Gospel relates, to pray by himself in an isolated place. When Peter and his companions realized that Jesus had gone, they quickly set out to find him.

As soon as they had caught up with him, they reported that he was the talk of the neighborhood and was being sought by everyone. Jesus' response was to suggest that they should all make their way to the country towns of Galilee in order to proclaim his message of salvation.

During Jesus' tour of this area, he met a man who was suffering from a skin disease. Mark does not specify the exact place of the incident, while Luke states that it happened in one of the towns. Matthew, however, says that it occurred after Jesus had come down from the mountain or hill near Capernaum

on which he had preached his "sermon on the mount." In any case, the three Gospels do broadly agree on what happened next.

A man suffering from a skin disease – some translations say he was a leper, although the original Greek, in which the New Testament was written, does not necessarily imply that he was – approached Jesus. Falling on his knees before Jesus, the man implored him with the words, "If you are willing, you can cleanse me." Jesus took pity on his suffering, stretched out his hand, and as he touched him, said, "I am willing. Be cleansed." In an instant, Jesus' healing power took effect and the skin disease was cured. As Jesus sent the man away, he told him sternly not to

Jesus heals the man with the skin disease in Matthew's account of the miracle. Jesus is shown walking down a hill, having just finished his "sermon on the mount." The illumination is from a German Bible made during the reign of Henry III (1017–56).

divulge to anyone about the miracle that he had just performed. Instead, he should go to the priest and "make the offering for your cleansing prescribed by Moses as evidence to them."

Here, Jesus was referring to the Jewish Law about skin diseases. According to this, people suffering from leprosy or other contagious skin diseases could not enter a house or associate with others. Instead, they had to wear torn clothing, keep their hair uncombed, and shout the words, "Unclean, unclean [Leviticus 13:45]."

If a person recovered from the disease, he or she had to go to the officiating priest in Jerusalem and make an offering, which included two clean live birds, cedar wood, scarlet fabric, and hyssop (Leviticus 14:4). By insisting on the legal purification ritual, Jesus was making it clear to any potential critics that he was working within the Jewish Law, and not flouting it.

† Signs of the Messiah †

But the man, exuberant as a result of his miraculous cure, could not keep his story to himself and proclaimed it to everyone he met. As a result, Jesus could not enter any town for fear of being mobbed, but confined himself to remote spots in the country. "Even so, people from all around kept coming to him."

Even at this early stage of his ministry, Jesus was concerned not to court undue publicity through his miracle-working. One of the signs of the Messiah, the "Anointed One" the Jews were expecting to come to lead them to salvation, was that he would perform miracles. No doubt Jesus realized early that his idea of messiahship was different from that of the common people.

They were looking for a strong, politically motivated, charismatic individual who would lead them to triumph against the occupying force of Rome. Jesus, by contrast, saw his messianic role in terms of leading sinners to a restored relationship with God and thereby establishing God's kingdom on Earth. ✦

MESSAGE
—for—
TODAY

ACCORDING TO the earliest manuscripts of Mark's Gospel, when the man with a skin disease approached Jesus, he was filled "with warm indignation." In later versions, scribes changed these words to "feeling sorry for him" because anger was felt to be incompatible with Jesus' character. Yet righteous anger — that is, anger based in God's truth and love — is not sinful. The church believes that Jesus was both fully divine and fully human. He may have been angry at the physical damage the skin disease was causing its victim or at the social isolation the man would have suffered.

Lepers still exist today. So, too, do societal "lepers" — victims of prejudice, such as some racial minorities or AIDS sufferers. These people need others to feel "warm indignation" at their pain and isolation and to stretch out a hand of friendship, God's love, to them.

The FAITH of FRIENDSHIP

CURING the PARALYTIC

MARK 2:1–12; MATTHEW 9:1–8; LUKE 5:17–26

> " *But as they could not get the man to him through*
> *the crowd, they stripped the roof over the place*
> *where Jesus was; and when they made an opening, they lowered*
> *the stretcher on which the paralytic lay.*
> *Seeing their faith, Jesus said to the paralytic,*
> *'My child, your sins are forgiven.'* "
>
> MARK 2:4–5

ALTHOUGH NEWS of Jesus' teachings and miracles had spread around Galilee, forcing him to seek out remote places to escape excessive attention, according to Mark and Matthew, he finally returned to the town of Capernaum, where he had begun his ministry. Here, he took up residence in a house and soon attracted crowds of people eager to hear him speak. Among these, according to Luke, were "Pharisees and teachers of the Law, who had come from every village in Galilee, from Judaea and from Jerusalem." They had clearly heard rumors about this new teacher who was causing such a stir and wanted to hear and test him out in person.

As Jesus began to preach to the assembled crowd, four men arrived at the house carrying a paralyzed companion. They soon found that there were so many people inside and outside the house that they could not break through to see Jesus. Undaunted, they climbed up onto the roof and began to strip it away.

The four men then lowered the paralytic, still on his stretcher, into the middle of the room where Jesus was preaching. And he, seeing their faith, said to the paralyzed man, "My child, your

The ruins of ancient Capernaum on the northwestern tip of the Sea of Galilee are shown in this aerial view. The remains of the synagogue with its marble columns can be seen at center. Capernaum was a busy fishing port at the time of Jesus, and it was here that he healed the paralytic. Jesus made the town his headquarters during his Galilean ministry, and it was also the home of the Apostles Matthew, Peter, Andrew, James, and John.

Greek text in mural:
ΠΗ ΗΟ ΘΝΟΟ· Κ ΙΡΟΙ ΗΚΡΟΕ ΒΟ ΤΟΡΑΥΤΧ Κ 7 ΕΙ ΙΩ ΙΔ ΙΓΔ ΕΟΙ

IC XC

sins are forgiven." In saying this, Jesus may have been acknowledging that the man's physical symptoms were directly connected to sinful acts unstated by the Gospel writers.

At the same time, Jesus was claiming that he had the divine power to forgive sins, and it was this claim that shocked the Pharisees and scribes. Thinking that he was being blasphemous – only God could forgive sins – they began to ask themselves how a man could talk in that way. But Jesus knew what they were thinking and

Jesus tells the paralytic to pick up his stretcher and go home, in this late medieval mural from the monastery of St. John Lampidistis in Cyprus. Early Christian art frequently featured the carrying of the stretcher because it was felt to provide proof that the cure had been effected.

challenged them. He asked them whether it was easier for him to tell the paralytic that his sins were forgiven or to command the man to pick up his stretcher and walk. In other words, Jesus implied that instead of publicly forgiving the man

his sins, he could have simply cured him. And in order to underscore his point and demonstrate that he, Jesus, as the Son of man, actually did have the power to forgive sin, he turned to the paralyzed man and said to him, "I order you: get up, pick up your stretcher, and go off home."

† Through the roof †

Immediately, the man raised himself up from his stretcher, picked it up, left the house, and went home. Everyone was astonished. Luke's Gospel records: "They were all astounded and praised God and were filled with awe, saying, 'We have seen strange things today.'" And Matthew's states that, "A feeling of awe came over the crowd when they saw this, and they praised God for having given such authority to human beings."

The story of the paralytic focuses clearly on the element of faith. For it was the determination

The roofs of Roman houses from the ruins of ancient Herculaneum, in modern Naples, Italy, show the type of clay tiles that, according to Luke, the paralytic's friends had to remove in order to gain entry to the house. Herculaneum was destroyed by a massive volcanic eruption of Mount Vesuvius in AD 79.

and faith of the paralyzed man and his four friends that enabled the healing to take place. Seeing their way barred by crowds, they took the only option open to them, namely the roof.

Here the accounts of Mark and Luke diverge slightly. In Mark's Gospel, the suggestion is that the roof was typical of an ancient Palestinian house and made of wood and plaster. Luke, however, adapting his version to a Greek or Roman house, says that the roof was made of tiles. In each case, the determination involved in creating an opening large enough to pass the paralytic through was the same.

The other important element to note in the story is the opposition of some Pharisees and scribes to Jesus, even at this early stage of his ministry. No ordinary mortal could forgive sins, they believed – only God could do that in response to repentance, prayer, and offerings. But Jesus proved his power to forgive sins by effecting the cure. The sight of the paralytic walking off with his stretcher was physical evidence that even Jesus' most blinded opponents could not deny.

✝ The Son of man ✝

When responding to the scribes, Jesus is said by the Gospel writers to have referred to himself as the "Son of man," an enigmatic phrase that occurs in the New Testament only in the Gospels, Acts, and Revelation. Biblical scholars continue to debate its meaning. In the Old Testament, "Son of man" occurs in some places – for example in the book of Ezekiel – simply as a synonym for "man," an ordinary mortal.

> 66 'I order you: get up, pick up your stretcher, and go off home.' And the man got up . . . and walked out in front of everyone. 99
>
> MARK 2:11–12

In the context of the book of Daniel, however, "Son of man" is used to represent the "holy ones of the Most High." This refers to the Jewish faithful who had been martyred for their beliefs before having "kingship" conferred on them.

In the early Christian church, the title Son of man suggested both the suffering and glory of Jesus. The use of the phrase, coupled with his power to heal and his clever response to their inner questionings about his action, might have alerted the scribes and Pharisees to the fact that Jesus was a serious challenge to their authority. ✦

MESSAGE
— for —
TODAY

IN CURING THE paralytic, Jesus used the concern and persistence of the paralyzed man and his friends to bring healing to someone who was unable to seek help by himself. It was when Jesus saw their faith that he said to the paralytic, "Your sins are forgiven," and cured him.

Some people have been so crippled, physically or psychologically, that their ability to relate to God or others has been damaged or even paralyzed. Their recovery may well need help from their friends to persist in overcoming obstacles — as the paralytic's companions did — and to offer care, acceptance, and prayer. Friends sometimes stop short because they are all too aware of their own limitations. The greatest hope offered in this story is the fact that faith only needs to bring people to God. God will do the rest.

A SOLDIER'S DEVOTION

The CENTURION'S SERVANT

MATTHEW 8:5–13; LUKE 7:1–10

> *When he went into Capernaum a centurion
> came up and pleaded with him.
> 'Sir,' he said, 'my servant is lying at home
> paralyzed and in great pain.'*
>
> MATTHEW 8:5–6

JESUS' HEALING of the servant of a centurion, a Roman soldier, is notable because it is the first occasion in the Gospels that Jesus uses his healing power in connection with a Gentile, instead of a Jew. The miracle is found only in the Gospels of Matthew and Luke, suggesting that they may have based their accounts on a common source, unknown to Mark, which scholars refer to as Q. In both versions, the healing occurred in the town of Capernaum after Jesus, on a nearby hill, had given his Sermon on the Mount, the central core of his teaching.

In Matthew's account, a centurion came up to Jesus in town and told him with emotion that his servant was paralyzed and suffering great pain. To this Jesus replied that he would go to the soldier's house and cure the sick man. However, the centurion, presumably aware that it was an act of ritual impurity for a Jew to go inside the house of a Gentile, said to Jesus that he was not worthy to have him enter his home. It would be enough, he said, for Jesus simply to "give the word" and his servant would be cured.

To elaborate on why he had faith in Jesus, the Roman then explained that he understood the nature of authority – he himself was one link in a chain of command that stretched above and below him: "I say to one man, 'Go,' and he goes; to another, 'Come here,' and he comes; to my servant, 'Do this,' and he does it." Jesus was astonished by the man's conviction in his power and declared that he had not met anyone in Israel with faith as great as his. He also added that many a Gentile would be welcomed into the kingdom of Heaven. The story ends with Jesus telling the centurion to return home, that his request would be granted because of his faith. At that moment, Matthew says, the servant was cured.

✦ A righteous Gentile ✦

Luke's version of the miracle resembles Matthew's in essentials, but differs in that the centurion did not meet Jesus face-to-face. Instead, he sent a number of "Jewish elders" – local dignitaries – to ask Jesus to come and heal his servant who was "near death." These intermediaries explained to Jesus that the centurion deserved Jesus' attention, since he was well disposed toward the Jewish religion and had built a synagogue in Capernaum at his own expense.

Jesus agreed to go to the soldier's home, but as he neared it, the centurion sent another messenger to say that he was not worthy to have Jesus enter his house or even to meet him. As in Matthew's account, Jesus expressed amazement at the faith of this soldier and healed his servant.

It was this cure of the centurion's servant that brought Jesus into contact, directly in Matthew and indirectly in Luke, with a representative of the occupying power of Rome. The standard unit of the Roman army at that time was the legion, which was a force of 6,000 men divided into sixty 100-man centuries, each of which was commanded by a centurion.

These officers, responsible for the morale and discipline of their units, were known for their toughness and reliability. They formed the backbone of the Roman military machine.

Jesus blesses the kneeling centurion, in this detail from a 19th-century stained-glass window in Lincoln Cathedral, England. In Luke's version of the story, Jesus does not actually meet the soldier in person, but learns of him through Jewish intermediaries.

Centurions are mentioned elsewhere in the New Testament, and on each occasion they are recorded in a positive light. It was, for example, a centurion who realized that the crucified Jesus was Son of God (Matthew 27:54). And the first Gentile convert to Christianity was a centurion

A SOLDIER'S DEVOTION ✦ 27

named Cornelius, who lived in the city of Caesarea (Acts 10). What distinguished the Capernaum centurion was his generosity, humanity, and humility. While some of his colleagues despised the Jews, he, like some other Gentiles – often called God-fearers – admired Jewish monotheism and its high moral teaching.

> 66 *When Jesus heard these words he was astonished at him and, turning round, said to the crowd following him, 'I tell you, not even in Israel have I found faith as great as this.'* 99
>
> LUKE 7:9

His attitude toward his servant, who would have been a slave, was unusually enlightened. In the Roman world, slaves had no rights and little or no protection against maltreatment. The Greek

philosopher Aristotle described a slave as a "living tool"; the Roman writer Varro equated slaves with cattle – the only difference being that they were articulate; and the Roman statesman and writer Cato once wrote that when buying a farm, the new owner should get rid of old or sickly slaves.

✦ A man of authority ✦

This centurion, however, was clearly concerned for the welfare of his servant – enough to petition Jesus to cure him. At the same time, he understood that a Jew was forbidden by religious Law to enter the house of a Gentile – a taboo that Peter later overcame when visiting the house of Cornelius (Acts 10:25–29). Yet the centurion's faith in Jesus' power was so great that he believed it was unnecessary for Jesus physically to touch his servant. He knew from his own

The synagogue at Chorazim, north of the Sea of Galilee, is one of the best preserved in Israel. It would have been a synagogue similar to this one that the centurion built for the people of Capernaum.

The aqueduct at Caesarea is one of the most impressive Roman monuments of Palestine. The seat of the Roman imperial government in the area for over 600 years, Caesarea featured a man-made harbor from which Saint Paul later made his final voyage to Rome.

military experience that if someone with authority gave a command, it was carried out; he recognized Jesus as a man of great spiritual authority and so was convinced that he would be able to implement actions simply by speaking the word.

The centurion's attitude made a deep impression on Jesus, prompting him, in Matthew's account, to say: "In truth I tell you, in no one in Israel have I found faith as great as this. And I tell you that many will come from east and west and sit down with Abraham and Isaac and Jacob at the feast in the kingdom of Heaven; but the children of the kingdom will be thrown out into the darkness outside, where there will be weeping and grinding of teeth."

Jesus was referring to the feast which, according to Jewish tradition, would inaugurate the coming of the messianic era (pp. 48–51). But instead of the "children of the kingdom" – that is, the Jews, the natural heirs to the kingdom of God – sitting down at this banquet with the three great Patriarchs of their tradition, it would be Gentiles "from east and west" taking their place. ✦

MESSAGE
—for—
TODAY

ACCORDING TO Luke – who wrote his Gospel primarily for Gentiles – the centurion, along with most of the Gentiles, never actually met Jesus face-to-face. Yet he had clearly been sufficiently impressed by Jesus' reputation to have faith in his healing powers.

Although there are those who have met influential spiritual teachers or have had decisive spiritual or conversion experiences, others come to faith more gradually. Through their profession, say as teachers, doctors, or farmers, some discover a pattern to life that points them to a belief in God. Others, like the centurion, find that their responsibility for the welfare of others leads them to recognize the importance of spiritual and moral values. Jesus made clear in his response to the centurion's faith that how a person comes to belief is ultimately less important than the way he or she shows that faith in daily life.

LORD of LIFE and DEATH

The SON of the WIDOW of NAIN

LUKE 7:11–17

> 66 *Then he went up and touched the bier and the bearers stood still, and he said, 'Young man, I tell you: get up.'* 99
>
> LUKE 7:14

A CCORDING TO the Gospel of Luke, some time after Jesus healed the centurion's servant, he traveled to the town of Nain, about 8 miles (13 km) southeast of Nazareth. Here, to the amazement of the townspeople, he performed the greatest of miracles – bringing the dead to life. Two other such instances are reported in the Gospels – the daughter of Jairus (pp. 44–47), and Lazarus, the brother of Mary and Martha (pp. 70–73).

In this case, Jesus had traveled to Nain in the company of his disciples and a large crowd of people, who probably had joined him from towns and villages in the local area. He had gotten as far as the gate of the town when he saw a funeral procession. The deceased was the only son of a widow – Luke does not record her name.

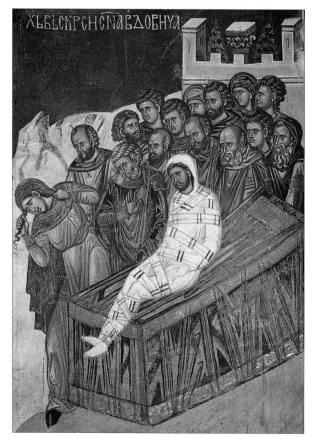

When Jesus saw the widow, he was filled with compassion and went over to comfort her. Then he approached the funeral bier and touched it – to come in contact with the body itself would, by Jewish Law, have rendered him ritually impure for a period of seven days. While those carrying the bier came to a halt, Jesus addressed the corpse, telling the man to get up. At once, the man sat up and started speaking, and "Jesus gave him to his mother." The astonished onlookers responded to this by hailing Jesus as a great prophet.

The miracle at Nain – which Luke understood to reveal Jesus as lord of both life and death – arose from Jesus' impulsive feeling of

The widow of Nain tugs her hair with emotion as her son is raised from the dead, in this 14th-century Serbian mural.

pity for the widow. Luke captures the drama of the incident by describing the dead man suddenly sitting up and beginning to talk. Jesus' power was sufficient not only to restore life to the dead, but also instantly to revive movement and speech.

✝ The widow of Zarephath ✝

Luke may have intended to link this event with the Old Testament episode in which the prophet Elijah also raised from the dead a widow's son (1 Kings 17:17–24). In this story, which is set against the background of a severe drought, Elijah was taking shelter in the home of a widow in the town of Zarephath. While he was staying there, her son died.

Elijah, praying fervently to God, managed to bring the boy back from the dead and then "gave him to his mother." The Greek translation of this phrase from the original Hebrew is the same as that used by Luke in his account. And the woman responded to the miracle by acclaiming Elijah as a "man of God."

Luke reports this miracle, as well as that of the healing of the centurion's servant, just before he describes John the Baptist sending messengers to Jesus. John's messengers asked him whether he was the "one who is to come," that is, the Messiah (7:19–22). Jesus told them to go back to John and tell him that "the blind see again, the lame walk, those suffering from virulent skin-diseases are cleansed, and the deaf hear, *the dead are raised to life* [author's italics] …"

By his reply, Jesus affirmed that, indeed, he *was* the Messiah; his words would have reminded John of the signs of the messianic age stated in the book of Isaiah: "Then the eyes of the blind will be opened, the ears of the deaf unsealed, then the lame will leap like a deer [35:5]."

In other words, Jesus' raising of the widow's son was, like his other healings, a physical manifestation of his teachings. In word and deed, Jesus displayed both the spirit and power of God and the inauguration of the messianic age. ✦

MESSAGE
—for—
TODAY

ALTHOUGH IT WAS the widow's son to whom Jesus restored life, Luke focuses his account on the plight of the distraught mother. In his compassion, Jesus first went over to her and sympathized with her distress over the loss of her only son.

Christians believe that their loved ones who die will be raised to new life in the next world, but this hope does not always diminish the immediate pain of loss. Jesus showed that it is appropriate to allow the bereaved to express their grief. Even if the promise of resurrection is, for Christians, the ultimate consolation, to someone who is in the first shock of bereavement, giving words of sympathy or a shoulder to cry on is a Christlike act of caring, and may be of the greatest comfort to them.

MASTER of the ELEMENTS

CALMING the STORM at SEA

MARK 4:35–41; MATTHEW 8:23–27; LUKE 8:22–25

*"And leaving the crowd behind they took him, just as he was,
in the boat; and there were other boats with him.
Then it began to blow a great gale and the waves were breaking
into the boat so that it was almost swamped. "*

MARK 4:36–37

T HE SEA OF Galilee is a large freshwater lake in northern Palestine, lying about 700 feet (200 meters) below sea level. It was here that Jesus, as related by the Synoptic Gospels – those of Mark, Matthew, and Luke – astonished his disciples by calming a storm. According to Mark, as Jesus was teaching by the shores of the lake, so huge a crowd gathered that he and his disciples had to get into a boat and preach to them from the water. When evening came, he suggested to his disciples that they cross over to the other side of the lake.

Matthew and Luke, whose accounts are slightly less detailed than Mark's, imply that Jesus and his companions were alone. Mark, however, mentions other boats, possibly those of fishermen or vessels filled with people eager to hear Jesus' teaching. Soon after they had set sail, a great gale began to blow, whipping up the surface of the lake. Waves buffeted the boat, then broke over its side, swamping it with water. Despite the hiss of frothing waves and, undoubtedly, the shouts of his companions, Jesus remained at the back of the boat, "his head on the cushion, asleep."

Terrified by the imminent threat of drowning and alarmed by Jesus' seeming indifference to their perilous predicament, the disciples roused him from his sleep with the words: "Master, do you not care? We are lost!" In Matthew's account, the disciples are shown in a more sympathetic light; they simply exclaim, "Save us, Lord, we are lost!" Waking up, Jesus quickly saw what was happening and "rebuked" the wind and said to the sea "Quiet now! Be calm!" Immediately, the gale dropped and the lake became calm.

† The lord of water and wind †

A s the disciples regained their composure, Jesus asked them why they were so frightened and pointed out their lack of faith. For their part, the disciples were "overcome with awe" – despite the fact that they had roused him precisely so that he would act to save them. Yet Jesus' action had shaken their perception of who he was. "Who can this be?" they said to one another. "Even the wind and the sea obey him."

Calming the storm at sea is the first nature miracle recounted in the Synoptic Gospels. These miracles have always attracted more controversial debate than healing miracles, since they seem to constitute more of a violation of natural laws. Jesus' taming of the storm is no different.

One popular rationalistic interpretation of the story is that Jesus and his disciples were actually caught in a sudden storm on one occasion, but that Jesus' reassuring presence and confident assertion that the winds would soon abate later

The boat *carrying Jesus and his disciples is rocked by waves, in this painting*
by the 19th-century British artist John Martin. In the background, Martin
has depicted a Palestinian town in the style of an ancient Greek city-state.

led the disciples to believe – after the storm had died down naturally – that he had caused them to do so. But the idea of God having power over the forces of nature is a familiar theme in the Bible. In the Old Testament, for example, God parted the "sea of reeds," to allow the Israelites to escape the pursuing Egyptians. And in the Psalms, God is said to "calm the turmoil of the seas, the turmoil of the waves [65:7]." In another psalm, God "rescued them [sea voyagers] from their plight, he reduced the storm to a calm, and all the waters subsided, and he brought them...to the port where they were bound [107:28–30]."

The Sea of Galilee was the scene of Jesus' stilling of the storm. About 12 miles (19 km) long and 8 miles (13 km) wide at its greatest extent, the lake is still plied by the boats of fishermen.

In the Talmud, a collection of rabbinical teachings, a rabbi named Gamaliel was traveling in a ship when a huge wave threatened to wreck it. The rabbi prayed to God and the raging sea subsided.

✝ Weather magic ✝

In the disciples' day, there was also a strong tradition of "weather magic" outside the biblical world. The Greeks, for instance, believed that the prayers of the people of Delphi summoned winds that hampered the Persian king Xerxes in his preparations to invade Greece in 480 BC. The Seleucid king Antiochus II (c. 287–246 BC) is said to have believed that he could control the waves of the sea. And the Roman statesman Cicero said of his countryman Pompey that winds and storms obeyed his will.

The disciples, alarmed by their predicament, wake Jesus, in this ninth-century German ivory relief. Mark says that Jesus was sleeping in the boat while the storm was raging.

To early Christian readers, Jesus' successful "rebuking" of the storm would have seemed an extraordinary and powerful action, but one that was not unfamiliar. They would also have recognized the manner in which Jesus dealt with the natural elements. For it was a common belief of the time that storms, gales, and tumultuous waves and other natural phenomena were due to the action of demonic spirits. As a result, Jesus exorcized the wind and waves as if they were possessed people.

> **❝ Why are you so frightened, you who have so little faith? ❞**
> MATTHEW 8:26

The point of the story as the Gospel writers intended it, however, was to show Jesus' control over the elements as further evidence of his divine power and authority. The story can also be read at a symbolic level. When the storms of life threaten to be overwhelming, even when faith in the saving power of God falters, the powerful presence of Jesus Christ will still be there, his ability to quell the winds and waves of misfortune an ever-present reality. ✦

MESSAGE
—for—
TODAY

THE DISCIPLES' faith in God's protection was quickly shaken by the first storm described in the Gospels. Like the disciples, many people of faith have known a moment of panic — perhaps when traveling in an aircraft during heavy turbulence.

Even more frightening can be the storms that rage within a person — fears of failure, loss, pain, or death. At such times, God may not seem to be near — as though God were sleeping. But when the tempest passes or panic subsides, God's presence often seems real again. Yet, as the disciples learned, even in the midst of a storm, God is present and will stretch out a guiding hand. In fact, God did much more than the disciples apparently expected. How different frightening times would be if people exercised their faith to watch for God's remarkable power at work.

CASTING DEMONS into SWINE

The GERASENE DEMONIAC

MARK 5:1–20; MATTHEW 8:28–34; LUKE 8:26–39

> 66 *Then he asked, 'What is your name?' He answered,*
> *'My name is Legion, for there are many of us.'* 99
> MARK 5:9

A FTER JESUS HAD stilled the storm on the Sea of Galilee, he and his disciples landed on the eastern side of the lake in an area called, according to Mark and Luke, the territory of the Gerasenes. In Matthew it was the Gadarenes. Mark and Luke, whose versions of the story are twice as long as Matthew's, state that as soon as Jesus stepped out of the boat a man possessed with devils, or with an "unclean spirit," came toward him.

This stranger must have presented a disconcerting sight. The Gospels relate that his illness was so disturbing that he had been forced to live away from human habitations and eke out an existence living naked among tombs. There, the people of his city had tried to tie and chain him up, but all forms of restraint had failed.

In fact, although the treatment of the wretched man may seem cruel, it is probable that the chains were intended to prevent him from harming himself as much as anyone else. Mark relates that the demoniac roamed among the tombs and the nearby mountains, howling and gashing himself with stones.

The possessed man was presumably watching Jesus' boat approach the shore. He seemed to know instinctively who was disembarking, since without a moment's hesitation, he ran up to Jesus and fell at his feet. Jesus, it seems, immediately divined what was wrong with the man and began to perform an exorcism, ordering the unclean spirit to come out of him. This prompted the man to shout out at the top of his voice: "What do you want with me, Jesus, son of the Most High God? In God's name do not torture me!"

✦ A legion of evil spirits ✦

Jesus then asked the man what his name was, a request that recalls the prevailing belief that a person's name had a power of its own, and that to gain control of someone it was necessary to know his or her name. "Legion," replied the demoniac. Taking the name of a Roman military unit points to the fact that he had been possessed not by one, but by an army of unclean spirits.

In Mark's account, the man implored Jesus not to send the spirits out of the district. But in Luke, the spirits themselves spoke to Jesus, begging him not to consign them to the "Abyss" – the realm where, in the book of Revelation, the fallen angels were imprisoned until their final judgment.

Before Jesus could respond to their entreaty, the spirits suggested where they should be sent. On a mountainside nearby grazed a large herd of pigs. The devils begged Jesus to send them into the pigs. Jesus consented, and the spirits left the man and entered the animals. The effect was dramatic. The

herd – about 2,000 strong – "charged down the cliff into the lake and was drowned."

The swineherds who had been looking after the pigs were filled with consternation. They immediately ran off to their hometown and to other places in the vicinity to recount the amazing events they had witnessed. Very soon,

Under the stern gaze of Jesus, a winged devil flies out of the Gerasene demoniac, who is nuzzled by docile-looking pigs, in this medieval ivory relief.

people came from all around to see and hear for themselves what had actually taken place. When they reached Jesus, they found the demoniac sitting quietly at his feet. Their immediate reaction was fear, presumably because Jesus had not only been powerful enough to transform the demoniac, but also because he had been prepared to sacrifice a large herd of pigs in the process. So they begged Jesus to leave their neighborhood, and Jesus agreed to their request.

✦ In Gentile country ✦

Just as Jesus was getting into his boat, the cured demoniac came up to him and asked to be allowed to go with him. But Jesus replied that he wanted him to stay where he was and tell everyone what God had done for him. In Mark's account, the man went home to the Decapolis. This was a confederation of ten cities, mostly Gentile in character, almost all of which lay east of the Jordan in Galilee. Luke simply states that he went to his home city.

The exorcism of the Gerasene demoniac is one of the more puzzling incidents in the Gospels. Although the Gospel writers broadly agree about

Columns from a Byzantine church are the best-preserved ruins of Gadara, situated in present-day Jordan. According to Matthew, it was the Gentile area around this town that provided the setting for the miracle.

the story, they differ in details. Matthew, for example, states that there were two demoniacs, not one. He also places the incident in the country of the Gadarenes, that is, the area around the town of Gadara. But this lay not on the lakeside, but 6 miles (10 km) to the southeast. Mark and Luke say it took place in the country of the Gerasenes, but Gerasa was about 30 miles (50 km) away from the lake. Certainly the area seems to have been a Gentile neighborhood because of the presence of pigs, considered unclean by Jews.

> ❝ *And the herd charged down the cliff into the lake and was drowned.* ❞
> LUKE 8:33

The demoniac's name, Legion, with its association with Rome, also points to a Gentile environment. Indeed, one modern scholar, seeking a rationalistic explanation, has stated that the story may be connected with the fact that one Roman Legion, the Tenth, was stationed in Galilee between 70 and 135 AD, not far from the locale of the story. This legion's emblem was a wild boar, so possibly the story originated in a nationalistic desire to be rid of the Roman "pigs."

*A **boar**, shown in this Roman mosaic, was the emblem of the Tenth Legion. The miracle story may be linked with the Jews' desire to eject the legion from Palestine.*

The crux of modern scholars' unease about the miracle is the fact the Jesus was apparently prepared to sacrifice a herd of pigs – without a thought for the financial loss to its owner. One modern interpretation suggests that when the man was being exorcized, his screams threw the nearby herd into panic, which led onlookers to believe the pigs had become possessed by his unclean spirits. On the other hand, Jesus may have been making the point that the saving of one person's sanity was worth the lives of 2,000 pigs, although this possibility has been strongly criticized by those involved in animal welfare.

In any case, the effect of Jesus' exorcism could not have been more dramatic or failed to have attracted the attention of those living in the area. And it is perhaps not surprising that, as the Sea of Galilee washed ashore the corpses of dead swine, the local people wanted to see the back of this mysterious and powerful rabbi. The cured demoniac did not, however. His plea to accompany Jesus flatly turned down, he was given the task to spread the word and testify to the power of God in this Gentile territory. ✦

MESSAGE
— for —
TODAY

THE GERASENES had clear evidence of Jesus' power to free a person from demons. Yet, rather than ask Jesus for further help, they begged him to go away. Perhaps they feared that in securing the spiritual welfare of others, Jesus would require them to suffer further material losses.

Today, there are many instances in which spiritual welfare and material wealth seem to face off in society. Someone seeks to establish a group home for troubled youths, and residents nearby sign petitions to prevent it, lest their property values fall. A church tries to open a shelter and soup kitchen and local businesses revolt.

Jesus apparently placed far greater value in one person's spiritual salvation than in a valuable investment. Would the world be a different place if more people, in faith, could do the same?

A TOUCH of FAITH

JAIRUS' DAUGHTER ✦
The WOMAN with HEMORRHAGES

MARK 5:21–43; MATTHEW 9:18–26;
LUKE 8:40–56

**❝ *My little daughter is desperately sick.
Do come and lay your hands on her that she
may be saved and may live.* ❞**

MARK 5:23

AFTER HIS ENCOUNTER with the Gerasene demoniac, Jesus again crossed the Sea of Galilee and landed on its western shore near Capernaum. Mark and Luke relate that as soon as he had landed, he was surrounded by a large crowd, which confined him to the margin of the lake. One of those gathered there was a man named Jairus, who was the president of a synagogue – an important official responsible for the arrangements of worship. Jairus broke through the crowd, came up to Jesus, and fell at his feet, begging him to come to his house to heal his daughter. According to Mark, the girl was "desperately sick," while Luke says she was dying. Matthew's version of the story, which is more abbreviated, states that the girl had just died.

Without delay, Jesus set off with Jairus, closely followed by a crowd of people. Among them was a woman who had suffered from hemorrhages, or an issue of blood, for twelve years. Mark says that she had gone to various doctors and spent all her money on long and painful treatments, but had continued to get worse. Luke states that no one had been able to heal her, but omits Mark's pejorative comment about the doctors, perhaps because, as tradition has it, he was a doctor himself.

The woman had heard stories of Jesus' power to heal and believed that if she merely touched Jesus' clothes, or the fringe of his cloak, as Matthew puts it, she would be healed. This she duly did and immediately "the source of the bleeding dried up," and she knew the cure had been effected. But the woman's hopes of doing it unnoticed failed. Jesus realized that someone had touched his person because "power" had gone out of him. Immediately, he turned around, faced the crowd, and demanded who had touched him. Denials rang out from the crowd, and Peter pointed out to him that there were so many people around him that it could have been anyone.

✝ *Saved by faith* ✝

But Jesus knew that someone had touched him not by accident, but with intent. So he stared at the sea of bemused faces, looking to see who had done it. The tension was too much for the woman to bear. She came forward "frightened and trembling," perhaps because she was ashamed of her surreptitious act or because she knew that her condition made her, by Jewish Law, ritually impure. Falling at Jesus' feet, she declared to him and the expectant crowd the whole truth. Jesus simply replied that her faith had healed or "saved" her.

Meanwhile, even as Jesus was talking to the woman, people arrived from Jairus' house bearing bad news. They told Jairus that his daughter was

dead, and that there was no point in troubling Jesus further. But Jesus overheard their words and told the president not to be afraid, only to have faith. With that, he went off alone with Peter, James, and John and entered Jairus' house. Immediately, he was struck by the noise and weeping of the mourners.

Jesus stopped the noise with the words: "Why all this commotion and crying? The child is not dead, but asleep." This provoked ridicule among the mourners, so to prove his point, Jesus went

Jesus awakens the daughter of Jairus, in this Christian relief from the so-called Sarcophagus of the Apostles in Pain. The relief, which is housed in Arles Museum, France, dates from the fourth century.

to where the girl was lying and, according to Mark, said to her, "*Talitha kum!*" – a phrase in Aramaic, Jesus' native language, meaning "Little girl, I tell you to get up." At once, the girl rose from her bed and began to walk around, astonishing her parents and everyone else present.

Falling on her knees, the woman with hemorrhages reaches out to touch the hem of Jesus' cloak, in this 14th-century Byzantine mosaic from a church in Istanbul, Turkey.

Jesus then forbade anyone to tell what had happened and instructed that the girl should be given something to eat.

The stories of Jesus' healing of Jairus' daughter and the woman with hemorrhages hinge on faith. In the first instance, the fact that Jesus was confronted by a senior synagogue official is significant. The Gospels frequently mention the growing conflict between Jesus and the religious authorities, and contrast it with Jesus' popularity with the common people. But here it is an important member of the religious establishment who sought Jesus' help, prepared even to abase himself at Jesus' feet in public. His conviction must have impressed Jesus.

At this point in Mark and Luke, the story is interrupted by the woman with the hemorrhages. Like Jairus, she saw Jesus as her last hope – Mark

relates her painful experiences with the medical profession. Her illness, which seems to have been menorrhagia, a continuous menstruation, was not uncommon, and various treatments for it were prescribed in the Talmud, some of which may have been practiced at the time of Jesus. These ranged from astringents and tonics to more bizarre practices, such as carrying the ashes of an ostrich egg in a linen rag. In any case, all remedies had failed and Jesus was her last chance.

✝ *"Your faith has healed you"* ✝

When the woman touched Jesus' robe, he felt power leave his body. "Power" is a translation of the Greek word *dunamis*, a term used by pagan worshipers in the Greco-Roman world to describe a supernatural force, usually conceived as an impersonal energy. But what distinguishes the Gospel accounts from a pagan miracle story is the fact that Jesus was fully conscious of his sudden drain of energy – he went on to establish a personal contact with the woman and emphasize her faith. He did not want her to slip away unnoticed – the healing had to be confirmed, its full efficacy, it seems, only obtainable after the woman had told Jesus the whole truth.

The woman with hemorrhages might have been treated with contemporary Roman surgical instruments such as these. They include spatulas, tweezers, a probe, and a hook.

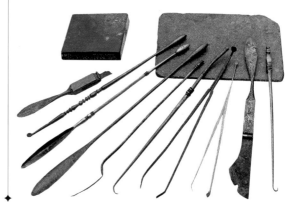

When Jesus told her that her faith had healed her, he was making the point that, in contrast to medical remedies, which only treated the body, her attitude of faith toward him had cured her both physically and spiritually – in fact, the Greek phrase "Your faith has healed you" could also be translated, "Your faith has saved you."

> " *And at once the source of the bleeding dried up, and ... she was cured of her complaint.* "
>
> MARK 5:28–29

The woman's faith in Jesus is mirrored by that of Jairus. When messengers from Jairus' household arrived to say his daughter was dead, Jairus seems to have been ready to accept Jesus' encouragement. There is no report of his breaking down with emotion; he simply followed Jesus to his home. There, they encountered a typical scene of Jewish mourning.

Certain rules were laid down for this, including wailing and the rending of garments. Even the poorest Jew was expected to hire flute players and at least one professional mourner. So, for someone of Jairus' status, the noise and commotion emanating from his house must have been substantial. Clearly, no doubt existed in the mourners' minds that the daughter was dead.

Jesus dismissed the mourners, saying that the child was not dead, but asleep. Some scholars take this literally and believe that the child had been wrongly diagnosed – that she was not dead, but in a trancelike state, or coma. But most believe that Jesus was equating sleep with death.

The word for sleep in Greek was often used as a euphemism for death. And if the Gospel writers had not believed the child was raised from the dead, it is unlikely they would have included the story in their accounts. Jesus' words seem to indicate that the child was not dead beyond the point of recall, and this he proved by "waking her," restoring her to life. ✦

MESSAGE
—for—
TODAY

JAIRUS WAS an important man and might understandably have despaired at the delay that prevented Jesus from reaching his house before his daughter died. Also, Jesus could have been expected to give a religious leader preferential treatment over a poor "unclean" woman. Yet, Jesus treated the one as equal to the other.

People's problems can blind them to others' needs. In a hospital, for example, those waiting for treatment often are inclined to view their needs as more pressing than those of others in front of them. People of faith can forget that God has a larger view and the power to help. Jairus waited his turn, and both he and the woman refused to let other people get in the way of their confidence in God. Such confidence can empower people in a crisis to maintain compassion and perspective, even to the point of heroic action.

The LIVING WATER

The SICK MAN *at the* POOL *of* BETHESDA
JOHN 5:1–18

> *Now in Jerusalem next to the Sheep Pool there is*
> *a pool called Bethesda in Hebrew…*
> JOHN 5:2–5

ACCORDING TO John's Gospel, Jesus at some point in his ministry journeyed from Galilee to Jerusalem in order to celebrate a festival. It may have been Shavuot, or Pentecost, a harvest festival that also commemorated the giving of the Law at Mount Sinai, which every Jewish adult male was expected to attend. While he was in Jerusalem, Jesus went to the Pool of Bethesda, also known as Bethsaida, where "crowds of sick people" gathered. The attraction of the pool is explained in a verse omitted from some translations of the New Testament because it is thought to be a later addition. In this verse (5:4), it was said that the angel of the Lord would at certain times come down into the pool and disturb the surface of the water. After this, the first person to enter the pool was cured of any illness.

As Jesus stood among the blind and the lame, he spotted a man lying on a mat who had been ill – the Gospel does not say with what – for 38 years.

Jesus asked the man directly, "Do you want to be well again?" Some scholars think that by asking this, Jesus could have been questioning the man's desire to be healed. It is likely that he was crippled or paralyzed in his legs. The long duration of his illness may have made it such a way of life for him that a dramatic, albeit positive, change would have threatened his relatively stable, if handicapped, existence.

† Restored to health †

The man did not reciprocate Jesus' directness with a straight, "Yes, I want to be well." He answered simply that he had no one to place him in the pool when it became disturbed. His reply evidently satisfied Jesus, who told the man to

After he had cured the sick man, Jesus met him again at the Temple, the only remains of which are the Western Wall, shown here in the center.

"Get up, pick up your sleeping-mat and walk around." At once, the man took up his mat and tried out his restored mobility around the pool. John does not mention either gratitude from the man or surprise from the other sick people – perhaps, to deflect attention from himself, Jesus carried out the healing as discreetly as possible.

John adds another dimension to his account when he relates that the incident took place on the Sabbath. According to Jewish Law, the Sabbath was a day of rest, and the carrying of a burden was forbidden. This is expressed, for example, in the Old Testament book of Nehemiah (13:15); in that case, the burdens,

Amid a crowd of sufferers and their attendants, Jesus asks the sick man whether he wants to be well again, in this painting by the 17th-century Spanish artist Murillo.

which included wine, grapes, and figs, were clearly intended for commercial transactions. When some bystanders – obviously strict adherents of the Law – saw the man carrying his mat, they rebuked him. He excused himself by saying that he had simply obeyed the person who had cured him. When pressed as to who this was, he was unable to answer.

The account of the miracle does not end there, however. For Jesus soon afterward went to the Temple, where he met the man he had cured. He told him, "Now you are well again, do not sin any more, or something worse may happen to you." The man must have asked Jesus who he was, because he then returned to the Jews who had chastised him for carrying his mat and told them Jesus' name. His motive for doing so is unclear.

The result was that "the Jews began to harass Jesus" for this and other unnamed actions carried out on the Sabbath. Jesus responded by facing up to them with the words: "My Father still goes on working, and I am at work, too." Although the Sabbath was the traditional day of rest, in remembrance of God's rest after his creation of the universe, Jesus seems to say that neither God's creative energy, on which the world depends, nor his compassion and mercy ever ceased.

This point was reiterated by the Jewish philosopher Philo of Alexandria (c. 20 BC–AD 50),

The ruins of the Pool of Bethesda, where sick people gathered in the hope of a miracle cure, are located in the old part of Jerusalem and are shown here from above.

who said that in the same way that it is the nature of fire to burn and snow to be cold, God "never ceases doing," he "goes on working." So Jesus claimed that he was the Son of the Father, and his healings were acts of compassion that, by their nature, did not transgress the Sabbath laws. His response only enraged the Jews further. In their eyes, Jesus added to his sin of Sabbath-breaking that of blasphemy – equating himself with God.

✝ Healing and sin ✝

The sick man's healing at the Pool of Bethesda has similarities to the healing of the paralytic (pp. 22–25). In both accounts, a sick person is told to get up, pick up his stretcher or sleeping mat, and walk; the healing and forgiveness of sin are linked; and the result is a conflict with the Jewish authorities – the scribes and Pharisees in the case of the paralytic, and unnamed Jews in John's account. John, however, does not stress the element of faith, but rather the importance of the sick man's desire to be healed.

Some scholars have pointed out that John's account might have allegorical elements. According to this view, the pool's five porticos, or porches, stand for the five books of the Jewish Law. In the same way that the porticos shelter the sick and lame, but do not heal them, so the Law provides a framework for everyday life, but not a means for spiritual transformation. The 38 years of the man's illness equals the length of time that the Israelites wandered in the desert before they eventually reached the Promised Land (Deuteronomy 2:14). In both cases, there are many years of physical and spiritual suffering before deliverance by God or his representative.

> 66 *Now you are well again, do not sin any more, or something worse may happen to you.* 99
> JOHN 5:14

The water in the story may also be symbolic. In John's Gospel, Jesus distinguishes between ordinary water and the water of the Spirit, which, if drunk, will become "a spring of water, welling up for eternal life" (4:14). Here, it seems as if Jesus has taken the place of the angel that disturbed the surface of the pool and, as the "living" water, effected the healing at a spiritual, as well as a physical, level.

The connection between these two aspects of the illness is brought out when Jesus encountered the man in the Temple. When he told him to sin no more or "something worse may happen to you," Jesus was not necessarily implying that he thought the man's condition was originally caused by his sins. But he does suggest that the man should not take his healing for granted. Jesus' aim was to bring people to a new life in God, and the signs of their acceptance were both spiritual and physical well-being. If the man, having been healed, flouted the inner transformation and sinned, he would then be worse off than before. ✦

MESSAGE
—for—
TODAY

CHANGE CAN be frightening. Some people may even prefer the security of a bearable illness to the challenge of renewed health. After 38 years of living on the alms of pilgrims, it might have seemed easier to the sick man to continue in this way. Jesus acted only when he was convinced the man wanted to be healed.

Jesus' critics were also afraid of change. By concentrating on religious externals, they neglected the chance for spiritual renewal that observance of the Sabbath was meant to encourage. When religion becomes a matter of external routine, it can become a barrier rather than the gateway to new life. Elsewhere, Jesus emphasized the need for faith. Here, he stressed that a person must want to be healed, to seek the change for new life that God is ready to enact.

A MIRACULOUS FEAST

The FEEDING of the 5,000

MARK 6:30–44; MATTHEW 14:13–21;
LUKE 9:10–17; JOHN 6:1–13

❝ *So as he steppped ashore he saw a large crowd;*
and he took pity on them because they
were like sheep without a shepherd, and he set himself
to teach them at some length. ❞

MARK 6:34

O NE OF THE best known of Jesus' miracles, the feeding of the 5,000, is the only one that is told in all four Gospels. Another account of a feeding of a multitude also appears in Mark (8:1–10) and Matthew (15:32–39), and many scholars believe both stories are based on the same incident.

In Mark, the feeding of the 5,000 occurred after Herod Antipas, the ruler of Galilee, had ordered the execution of John the Baptist, who had condemned Herod for marrying his brother's wife. Before then, Jesus had visited his hometown of Nazareth. There he had been received with hostility, but had nonetheless sent out his 12 disciples to teach and heal in the area.

When the disciples had returned to Jesus and told him everything they had accomplished, he decided that they should go to a "lonely place" to recuperate from the rigors of their missionary work and escape the crowds they were attracting. So they took a boat and sailed off across the Sea of Galilee to a deserted spot – the Gospels do not say exactly where. However, Jesus' plan for peace and quiet was thwarted. Many people had seen them leave by boat and set off by land to meet them when they disembarked. When Jesus put in to land, he was greeted by the very crowds he had sought to avoid.

Even so, Jesus pitied them, because, as Mark says, "they were like sheep without a shepherd." Accordingly, he taught and healed the people until late in the day. At this point, the disciples became anxious. Here they were in an isolated place with a large crowd of people – an estimated 5,000 souls – with no food and the day turning to evening. So they put it to Jesus that he should send everyone off to buy food. But Jesus replied that they themselves should give the people food.

The disciples were taken aback, saying that they would need 200 denarii – one denarius was the payment for a day's work by a laborer – to buy enough food for everyone. When Jesus asked how much food there was, the most they could come up with was five loaves of bread and two fish – courtesy, according to John, of a small boy.

✝ Blessing the food ✝

J esus did not seem disconcerted by these meager rations. First, he told the disciples to make everyone sit on the ground in groups of fifty. Then, he blessed the food, broke up the loaves and divided the fish, and gave it all to the disciples to distribute. Everyone ate to their hearts' content, and when the scraps of food were gathered up, they filled 12 large baskets.

Although the feeding of the 5,000 is one of the most spectacular of Jesus' miracles, it appears to have provoked the least reaction among the disciples and common people. Only in John's account does the crowd seem to realize that a miracle has been performed.

An expectant crowd watches as Jesus, with lilylike emblems adorning his halo, blesses the basket of five loaves and the plate of two fish before giving them to the disciples for distribution. This detail comes from a 16th-century stained-glass window in the lady chapel of the Church of St. Pierre at Dreux in Normandy, France.

This factor has prompted some scholars to suggest that the story does not actually record a miracle at all. Instead, they put forward rational explanations, one of the most popular being that the people had in fact brought food with them, but were too selfish to share it. By freely distributing the loaves and fish, Jesus inspired a spirit of generosity, and enough food was produced to feed everyone. Yet it is evident that the feeding was regarded by the four evangelists as a miracle; otherwise, it would hardly have been worthy of inclusion in their Gospel accounts.

✝ Manna from heaven ✝

The story also contains allusions that members of the early church would have recognized, which give it an extra resonance. The fact that Jesus was miraculously feeding a crowd in a lonely or, literally, "desert," place would have recalled the Old Testament account of Moses leading the Israelites through the desert toward the Promised Land. Because of their hunger, God sent "manna from heaven" to feed them (Exodus 16).

Jesus, therefore, would have seemed like the new Moses, able, through God's power, to feed the "new Israel." Indeed, after John's account of the miracle in his Gospel there follows a long discussion about Jesus being the "bread of life," in which the evangelist spells out the connection between Moses and Jesus.

A priest breaks consecrated bread during the Eucharist, or Mass – the service that is anticipated by Jesus' miraculous feeding of the 5,000.

The feeding also echoed the occasion when the prophet Elisha fed 100 men with 20 loaves of bread – "they ate and had some left over... [2 Kings 4:44]." And it would have brought to Jewish minds the idea of the "messianic banquet." In Jewish tradition, one of the signs that the Messiah was ushering in the new world order at the end of time was a "great banquet."

✝ A feast for everyone ✝

References to this feast appear in the Old Testament, for example, in Isaiah 25:6, which refers to God preparing a "banquet of rich food" on a mountain "for all peoples." And Jesus himself used the image in some of his teachings about the kingdom of God (Luke 14:15–24). In all accounts of the feeding except John's, Jesus' action of taking the bread, blessing it, then breaking it for distribution follows the traditional way a Jewish host would have begun a meal. Thus it is possible that Jesus wanted to convey the idea that he was presiding at a feast that foreshadowed the coming messianic banquet when, as the Messiah, he would again be their host. It was perhaps a realization of this symbolism, coupled with their excitement at the miracle, that made the people in John's account hail Jesus as "the prophet who is to come into the world." Jesus, John says, quickly realized that the multitude wanted to

A basket of loaves and two fish – with which Jesus fed the crowd – are shown in this mosaic in the Church of the Multiplying of the Loaves at el-Tabgha in Israel.

seize him and "make him king." Knowing that the people had misunderstood his intentions and were regarding him as a political savior, Jesus "fled back to the hills alone."

> " *Then he took the five loaves and the two fish, raised his eyes to heaven and said the blessing; then he broke the loaves and began handing them to his disciples to distribute...* "
>
> MARK 6:41

But if the feeding was a foretaste of the messianic banquet, it was also an anticipation of the Eucharist, or Mass, the service that commemorates the Last Supper. On this occasion, Jesus also blessed and broke the bread and distributed it. For the first Christians, the feeding linked the Old Testament with the New, Moses with Jesus. It also connected an actual historical event with the practice of worship in the church and the fulfillment of the messianic age. ✦

MESSAGE
— *for* —
TODAY

THE MIRACLE OF *the loaves and fish shows Jesus' compassion and power, but it also demonstrates human responsibility. The disciples were content to let the people go and forage for themselves, and quite possibly others in the crowd were prepared to hoard their own secret supplies of food. Jesus insisted on human participation in his powerful work.*

It can be easy to ignore or dismiss other people's needs by deferring personal responsibility and leaving others to take action. If, like the disciples, however, people act in faith to do what God asks; if, like the young boy in John's account, who offered five loaves and two fish, everybody makes a small contribution — whether of time, energy, or material assistance — then everyone may be "fed."

LORD *of the* SEAS

WALKING *on* WATER

MARK 6:45–52; MATTHEW 14:22–23;
JOHN 6:16–21

> *He was going to pass them by, but when they saw him walking
> on the sea they thought it was a ghost and cried out…*
>
> MARK 6:48–49

THE GOSPEL accounts of the feeding of the 5,000 (pp. 48–51) are immediately followed in Mark, Matthew, and John by another nature miracle: Jesus walking on water. After Jesus had fed the crowd with the five loaves of bread and two fish, he told his disciples to set off in their boat and make their way to the western shore of the Sea of Galilee.

In the meantime, he sent the crowds away and withdrew into the hills nearby to pray. John's account indicates that Jesus actually withdrew because he knew the people wanted to make him a king, presumably to lead them in a nationalist uprising against the Romans.

By the "fourth watch" of the night – that is, between 3 a.m. and 6 a.m. – the disciples' boat was far out on the lake. Jesus came to the shore and saw them struggling to row against a strong headwind in turbulent water. So he approached the disciples, walking on the lake. At the sight of him, the disciples cried out in terror, certain that the figure they saw must be a ghost. He responded with the words, "Courage! It's me! Don't be afraid."

According to Mark's account, Jesus then climbed into the boat, and, at precisely the same time, the wind died down – much to the bewilderment of the disciples. Matthew, however, relates that Peter called out to Jesus before he reached the disciples and said, "Lord… if it is you,

tell me to come to you across the water." When Jesus replied to him, "Come," Peter climbed over the side of the boat and began to walk over the lake toward Jesus.

The disciple's progress faltered, however, when the wind's strength distracted him. Gripped suddenly by fear, Peter began to sink into the waves and cried out to Jesus, "Lord… save me!" Jesus immediately stretched forward and caught him, reprimanding him with the words, "You have so little faith… why did you doubt?" As the two men climbed into the boat, the gale stopped blowing. The other disciples, amazed at what had occurred, then fell at Jesus' feet and exclaimed, "Truly, you are the Son of God."

✝ The "dumbfounded" disciples ✝

As he did when he stilled the storm at sea (pp. 32–35), Jesus demonstrated his mastery over the elements by walking on the water. Mark's version of the miracle – which some scholars believe should be read as a continuous narrative with the feeding of the 5,000 – emphasizes the disciples' lack of insight into the very nature of Jesus. The account records that they were "completely dumbfounded, because they had not seen what the miracle of the loaves meant; their minds were closed ."

Mark seems to be saying that in Jesus' ability to feed a whole crowd with only a few fish and

loaves the disciples should have recognized that Jesus was working with the power of God. As a result, they should not have been surprised that he also had the power to walk on water.

In the Old Testament, God is sometimes described as walking through or on the waves –

The disciples watch in wonder from their boat as Jesus rescues his disciple Peter from the tumultuous waves of the Sea of Galilee, in this painting by the 18th-century German artist Philipp Otto Runge. The incident took place, according to the Gospel accounts, in the early hours of the morning.

for example, in the book of Job: "He and no other has stretched out the heavens and trampled on the back of the Sea [9:8]." And Jesus, so the Gospels suggest, acted with divine authority.

✝ Peter: the Rock ✝

Only Matthew's account ends with this revealing story of Peter, the foremost of Jesus' disciples. Originally named Simon, he was renamed Cephas by Jesus – an Aramaic word whose Greek equivalent is Petros, or Peter, meaning "rock." When Jesus was accompanied by a small group of his followers, Peter was always

The present-day Church of St. Peter stands on the shore of the Sea of Galilee at el-Tabgha, near Capernaum. Built to jut out into the sea, the structure recalls Jesus' implication that Peter would be the rock on which the Christian community would be built.

among them. At the town of Caesarea Philippi, it was Peter who called Jesus the Messiah and was rewarded by Jesus saying to him, "On this rock I will build my community [Matthew 16:18]."

> ❝*Jesus called out… 'Courage! It's me! Don't be afraid.' It was Peter who answered. 'Lord,' he said, 'if it is you, tell me to come to you across the water.'* ❞
> MATTHEW 14:27–28

Peter demonstrated his trust and faith in Jesus when he requested the power to walk on the water. That his faith was the issue becomes clear when his confidence lapsed, causing him to sink and prompting Jesus to rebuke him for his lack of faith. Some scholars believe that Peter's failure of

Outspoken and impetuous, Peter was nonetheless foremost among the twelve disciples. On one occasion, Jesus said he would give Peter the "keys of heaven," an idea illustrated in this medieval Italian painting.

nerve and his salvation from the waves anticipates his later denial of Jesus after Jesus had been arrested (Matthew 26:69–75), as well as their subsequent reconciliation by the Sea of Galilee after Jesus' resurrection (John 21).

Apart from its portrayal of Peter, the story would have had powerful symbolic resonance to the first Christians. Just as the disciples had labored to make headway against a contrary wind, so the early Christians struggled to establish themselves against a hostile Roman government in the second half of the first century AD.

The reign of Nero (AD 54–68) was particularly savage: numbers of Christians were crucified and burned – some of whom were blamed by the emperor for starting a fire in the city. And it was during these years that Peter and the Apostle Paul were reputedly put to death in Rome. But if Jesus could walk across the dark water to save his disciples, the nascent church could hope that he would also rescue them in their hours of darkness. ◆

MESSAGE
—for—
TODAY

WHEN PETER'S FAITH was shaken by the force of the gale, Jesus rebuked him, making the cause of Peter's trouble utterly clear. Only then did Jesus save him.

Before he could assume responsibility for leadership of the early church, Peter had to learn to rely on God's strength. So it is with all who venture out in faith. People who take on new responsibilities, whether raising a family or chairing a committee, may – even if their faith is strong – succumb to paralyzing fears when the going gets tough. Peter's experience is a reminder that a panic in times of crisis often betrays a lack of trust in God's providential care. The heart of faith lies in the ability to let go of an excessive reliance on personal resources and allow God to provide the support.

The HEALING of a GENTILE

The SYRO-PHOENICIAN WOMAN'S DAUGHTER

MARK 7:24–30; MATTHEW 15:21–28

" *At once a woman whose little daughter had
an unclean spirit heard about him and
came and fell at his feet ... and she begged him to drive
the devil out of her daughter.* "

MARK 7:25–26

A T SOME POINT during his ministry – neither Mark nor Matthew specifies exactly when – Jesus left the region of Galilee and headed north to the territory around Tyre. This coastal settlement and its northern neighbor Sidon were the chief cities of the Phoenicians, who were renowned as skillful sailors and traders.

According to Mark, Jesus hoped to find anonymity in this Gentile territory but failed to pass unrecognized – an unknown woman approached him and threw herself at his feet. Mark describes her as a Syro-Phoenician (a Phoenician from Syria), while Matthew calls her a Canaanite. This was the name that was used to describe the ancient inhabitants of the region, but it was also sometimes applied, in a general way, to the Phoenicians.

In Matthew's version, Jesus was accompanied by his disciples, who urged him to do what the woman asked because they wanted to get rid of her – she had been following them around, shouting entreaties at them, and making a nuisance of herself. Jesus then told the woman that he had been sent "only to the lost sheep of the House of Israel" – that is, his mission was only to the Jews. In Mark, where Jesus is said to be by himself, the woman begged him to "drive the devil out of" her daughter.

Jesus turned to her and said: "The children should be fed first, because it is not fair to take the children's food and throw it to the little dogs." But the woman, not to be deterred, quickly replied: "Ah, yes, sir...but little dogs under the table eat the scraps from the children."

Her answer evidently impressed Jesus: she did not deny the priority of the children – the Jews – to the kingdom of God, but asserted that after the rich pickings had been consumed, there would still be enough leftover morsels to satisfy the needs of the non-Jew. As a result, Jesus told her that her plea had been answered – her daughter was cured: "For saying this you may go home happy; the devil has gone out of your daughter."

† Jesus in Gentile territory †

The healing of the Syro-Phoenician woman's daughter stands out as Jesus' only known miracle on behalf of a Gentile in Gentile territory. Some scholars have argued that Jesus' visited this region specifically for the Gentiles. Others believe that Jesus was escaping the pressure and hostility that his teaching and miracle-working had aroused in Galilee.

There, Herod Antipas, ruler of the region, had recently executed John the Baptist. When rumors reached him of Jesus' prophetic activities, he

A small black devil *is depicted leaving the daughter of the Syro-Phoenician woman as Jesus watches, in this medieval Byzantine mural.*

believed, according to Mark, that the Baptist had returned from the dead. It would have made sense for Jesus to lie low for a while.

As in the healing of the centurion's servant (pp. 26–29), the only other time that Jesus is reported to have rewarded the faith of a Gentile, Jesus demonstrated his power to heal from a distance when he cured the woman's daughter. At the same time, the miracle raises questions about Jesus' apparent attitude toward the Gentiles, when he referred to them as "dogs."

Although this was a common pejorative term used by Jews to describe Gentiles, many modern commentators feel that its use is out of character for Jesus. Others, however, point out that the Greek word written in the Gospels is a diminutive form. This lessens the force of the term "dog" – and this may even give a sense of affection to it. The woman's quick-witted reply certainly suggests some kind of rapport between the two of them.

The theological problem this incident raises centers around the nature of the church's mission: Was the Gospel intended for the Jews, first and foremost, or were the Gentiles meant to be included as well?

This major question was still being debated when Mark and Matthew wrote their accounts of the Gospel during the second half of the first century. At the time,

some Christians insisted that those Gentiles who wished to join the church had to convert to Judaism first. Paul, the Apostle, however, vigorously opposed this view, and the church eventually followed his lead.

† A share in God's kingdom †

Jesus certainly focused his primary attention on the Jews. He clearly indicated, however, that the Gentiles would also share in God's kingdom. After he had cured the centurion's servant, for example, Jesus said: "And I tell you that many will come from east and west and sit down with Abraham and Isaac and Jacob at the feast in the kingdom of Heaven [Matthew 8:11]." By this, he seems to have meant that Gentiles would receive salvation and take their seats with the great Jewish Patriarchs at the messianic banquet (pp. 48-51).

Jesus expected that after his resurrection the Gentiles would be fully welcomed into the kingdom of God. Matthew, in his Gospel, records these words of the risen Christ: "Go, therefore, make disciples of all nations; baptize them in the name of the Father and of the Son and of the Holy Spirit [28:19]."

Scholars find it significant that in the Gospels of both Mark and Matthew, the miracle immediately follows a debate

These Roman columns are evidence that the Phoenician city of Tyre – in Lebanon, 50 miles (80 km) north of Jerusalem – was incorporated into the Roman Empire in 20 BC.

Herod Antipas, shown on this contemporary coin, was the ruler who executed John the Baptist, and from whom Jesus may have been escaping by going to Tyre.

between Jesus and the Pharisees about ritual cleanliness. The Pharisees criticized Jesus because some of his disciples were eating food with unwashed hands, contrary to the ritual cleansing that pharisaic custom demanded. Jesus replied that evil thoughts and intentions were what made a person unclean: "Nothing that goes into someone from outside can make that person unclean; it is the things that come out of someone that make that person unclean. Anyone who has ears for listening should listen! [Mark 7:15]."

> ❝ *Then Jesus answered her, 'Woman, you have great faith. Let your desire be granted.' And from that moment her daughter was well again.* ❞
> MATTHEW 15:28

Jesus, as a Jew, technically committed an act of ritual impurity by associating with a woman who was a Gentile. This was another reason, perhaps, why the disciples in Matthew's account wanted him to send her away from them.

Yet far from dismissing her, Jesus talked to her, tested her faith, and finally rewarded her by curing her daughter. He backed up his words with his actions, showing in the most palpable way possible that cleanliness and uncleanliness come not so much from performing outward acts but from attitudes of the heart. ✦

MESSAGE
—for—
TODAY

IN HIS COMPASSION *for the Syro-Phoenician woman's daughter, Jesus apparently overstepped the immediate limits of his missionary work, as well as the traditional constraints that kept Jews and Gentiles apart.*

People in all walks of life operate according to boundaries and priorities, both personal and societal. Some are the result of human limitations. Others come from intolerance, greed, or hatred. Religious differences, such as those in Bosnia or Northern Ireland, continue to keep people apart today.

When Jesus "broke the rule" of ministering only to the Jews, he illustrated the most fundamental attitude of faith — that in God's eyes neither a person's creed, color, nor nationality matters.

HEARING GOD'S WORD

The HEALING of the DEAF MAN
MARK 7:31–37

"And they brought him a deaf man who had an impediment in his speech; and they asked him to lay his hand on him."
MARK 7:32

JESUS' STAY IN the region of Tyre remains largely a mystery – the Gospels give little detail, apart from the healing of the Syro-Phoenician woman's daughter (pp. 56-59). At some point, however, Jesus decided it was time to travel back toward Galilee. According to Mark, he set off from Tyre and went, via Sidon, toward the Sea of Galilee and the Decapolis – a region, mostly to the east of the Jordan River, dominated by a league of ten cities with a predominantly Hellenistic, or Greek, culture.

While Jesus was in this area, a group of people came up to him, leading a companion who was deaf and had a speech impediment. Apparently knowing Jesus' reputation as a healer, they asked him to lay his hand on the deaf man. Jesus did not answer them, nor did he perform the simple action they requested. Instead, he took the deaf man aside, away from the crowd. He then placed his fingers inside the man's ears, touched the man's tongue with his spittle, raised his eyes heavenward with a sigh, and said "*Ephphatha*" – an Aramaic word meaning "be opened."

Immediately, the man could hear and speak clearly. Jesus ordered the witnesses not to tell anyone what he had done. But as had often happened before, the more he insisted, the more they spread the story.

The healing of the deaf man took place in Gentile territory, like the miracle in Tyre. It is not made clear in the Gospel account, however, whether the deaf man was a Jew or a Gentile. Mark concentrates in detail on the way

Clad in a blue robe, Jesus heals the deaf man, in this 14th-century Byzantine mosaic. The medieval artist has emphasized the man's disability by showing him holding a walking stick.

in which Jesus performed the healing of the sufferer and the sense of awe and wonder it provoked in the crowd afterward.

Jesus used techniques practiced by other miracle-workers of the time. The Roman historian Tacitus recorded, for example, how Emperor Vespasian used his saliva to cure a blind man and a cripple.

It is known that some miracle-workers in the ancient world used foreign words as part of their ritual formulas and that translating these words might rob them of their efficacy. In his account, Mark actually quotes the original Aramaic command that Jesus gave to the deaf man. Some scholars have suggested that Mark not only wanted to quote Jesus' original expression, but also wished to preserve the power of the word *Ephphatha*, perhaps for the benefit of contemporary Christian healers.

† The messianic age †

The whole incident culminates in the final pronouncement of the crowd, whose admiration for Jesus was "unbounded." Those who witnessed the miracle said: "Everything he does is good, he makes the deaf hear and the dumb speak." With these words, Mark recalls the signs recorded in the Old Testament, for instance in the Book of Isaiah, that were associated with the coming of the messianic age: "Then the eyes of the blind will be opened, the ears of the deaf unsealed…and the tongue of the dumb sing for joy [35:5–6]."

That Mark was consciously echoing this passage is clear from the adjective he chose to describe the deaf man's speech impediment. He used the Greek word *mogilalos*, which occurs only in the New Testament or in the Greek version of the Old Testament to translate the Hebrew word for "dumb" in Isaiah 35:6. By linking the two passages together, Mark seems to imply that Jesus was fulfilling his messianic destiny foretold by the prophets of old. ◆

MESSAGE
—for—
TODAY

WHEN HE CURED the deaf man, Jesus used physical techniques similar to those of contemporary wonder-workers. Unlike the other healers, however, Jesus was empowered by God, a point Mark emphasizes when he records Jesus' heavenward gaze before the healing.

Modern medical practices differ very greatly from those of the ancient world. Yet despite the real benefits of laser surgery, pacemakers, and the other techniques and tools of today, the faithful believe that healing is still, ultimately, the gift of God. Some people think that God works his curative powers through the laying on of hands. Many hold that God works through the skill and devoted service of surgeons, doctors, and nurses. For all believers, confidence that God's loving care is always with them gives comfort and strength.

LIGHT *of the* WORLD

The MAN *born* BLIND

JOHN 9:1–41

❝ As he went along, he saw a man who had been blind from birth. His disciples asked him, 'Rabbi, who sinned, this man or his parents, that he should have been born blind?' ❞

JOHN 9:1–2

O N A SABBATH, during a visit to Jerusalem to attend the Feast of Tabernacles – which commemorated the Israelites' wilderness sojourn after Moses had led them out of Egypt – Jesus and his disciples came across a beggar who had been blind from birth. The disciples turned to Jesus and asked the reason for the man's blindness, whether it was due to his or his parents' sins.

Jesus replied that neither the man nor his parents had sinned; rather he was blind "so that the works of God might be revealed in him." Jesus then made a paste out of spittle and dust, applied it to the man's eyes, and told him to go and wash it off in the Pool of Siloam within the city.

The beggar did as Jesus commanded and was healed. The astonished locals, who were used to seeing him sit and beg for his living, asked him how he had gained his vision. He told them about the "man called Jesus" and the cure. In turn, they took him to the Pharisees, who, when they were told what had happened, were most concerned that the healing had taken place on the Sabbath, the day of rest.

The Pharisees began to argue among themselves. Some said that Jesus must be a sinner because he had not kept the Sabbath. Others protested that a sinner would not have the power to perform such a miracle. When they turned to the beggar and asked him what he thought of Jesus, the man said without hesitation, "He is a prophet." His reply infuriated the Pharisees. Hoping to find proof that the man had never been blind in the first place, they sent for his parents and questioned them.

† Disciples of Jesus and Moses †

The man's parents had heard that anyone caught acknowledging Jesus as the Messiah would be banned from the synagogue. Although they confirmed that their son had been blind from birth and now was able to see, they denied that they knew how this situation had come about. They further distanced themselves from the situation by saying that their son was old enough to answer for himself.

The Pharisees again sent for the beggar and urged him to admit frankly that Jesus was a sinner. The man said to them that whether Jesus was a sinner or not he could not tell; he knew only that whereas he had once been blind, he could now see. The Pharisees greeted the man's dogged refusal to denigrate Jesus with frustration and fury. They hurled abuse at him, accusing him of being a disciple of Jesus and at the same time asserting their own orthodoxy as disciples of Moses. But the beggar remained uncowed, marveling at the

way the Pharisees seemed to ignore the evidence before their eyes – that Jesus, with his power to cure blindness, was a man from God. Angry that this man should be preaching to them, the Pharisees "ejected him."

When Jesus heard that the beggar had been thrown out by the Pharisees, he found him and asked him, "Do you believe in the Son of man?" The beggar asked Jesus to tell him who this was so that he could believe in him. When Jesus replied that it was he, the beggar said, "Lord, I believe," and worshiped him.

Jesus applies a paste of spittle and dust to the eyes of the blind man, who appears in this medieval Greek fresco on the right, washing the paste off in the Pool of Siloam.

Although the Gospels relate that Jesus healed the blind during his ministry, this is the only recorded occasion on which he cured someone who had been blind from birth. The miracle raises the question about the relationship between sin and suffering. Contemporary Jews believed that sin caused physical ailments and that a person's illness or disability at birth might come from some

prenatal or parental sin. Jesus avoided the theological discussion and simply said that the disability was an opportunity for God's power of salvation to be made visible.

† Restoring sight †

The keynote of the story, as John makes clear, is Jesus' assertion that he is the "light of the world" and that he has come into the world "so that those without sight may see and those with sight may become blind." The miracle was not only the physical healing, but also the way in which the blind man progressively realized who Jesus was. At first, he referred to him as "the man called Jesus." In his first interrogation by the Pharisees, he stated unequivocally that Jesus was a prophet – a man inspired by the power of God. Finally, he again met Jesus, who asked him if he believed in the Son of man (a variant reading is "son of God") – a messianic title. When Jesus declared himself the Son of man, it was as if the

The Pool of Siloam is one of the oldest extant sites of Jerusalem – possibly dating from the time of King David (1010–970 BC) – and has supplied the city with water for centuries.

The Temple, shown in this model, was rebuilt by Herod the Great in about 20 BC. The blind man is thought to have been begging outside the Temple when Jesus cured him.

man's eyes had been opened again, but this time at a spiritual level: now he could see fully.

If the cure of the blind man symbolizes the gaining of spiritual insight, the Pharisees epitomize spiritual blindness. At first, they were baffled and divided about Jesus' action: his breaking the Sabbath made him a sinner; but how could a sinner heal a blind man? Accordingly, they became determined to find a flaw in the healed man's story.

They interrogated the man's parents, who proved unhelpful. Then they interrogated the man himself for a second time. But when they asked him to repeat exactly what Jesus had done to him, presumably hoping to hear some detail that would incriminate Jesus, the exasperated healed man retorted with irony: "Do you want to become his disciples yourselves?"

> **❝ So when the Pharisees asked him how he had gained his sight, he said, 'He put a paste on my eyes, and I washed, and I can see.' ❞**
>
> JOHN 9:15

The Pharisees were outraged by the man's seeming insolence and affirmed their allegiance to Moses. John contrasts these traditionalists, who were unable to perceive Jesus' spiritual status – even with the evidence literally staring them in the face – with the healed man. After the latter had confessed his belief in Jesus, some Pharisees approached Jesus and asked him whether he considered them to be "blind."

Jesus replied enigmatically: "If you were blind, you would not be guilty, but since you say, 'We can see,' your guilt remains." By this he seems to have meant that as self-confessed religious experts who claimed to see the truth, yet who considered Jesus to be a sinner, the Pharisees were actually guilty of true blindness. ✦

MESSAGE
—for—
TODAY

IN JOHN'S STORY of the cure of the man born blind, Jesus seems to suggest that sin is more likely to cause spiritual, rather than physical, blindness. Unlike some of his contemporaries, he hesitated to link physical illness with wrongdoing.

Today, many people still want to attribute suffering to some wrongdoing on the sufferer's part. Whether the illness appears as impoverishment, disease, disability, or ignorance, the implication that the sufferers are somehow to blame for their condition leads to cynicism and a profound lack of compassion. Yet such cynicism – like the Jewish leaders' attack on Jesus for curing the blind man on the Sabbath – is symptomatic of the spiritual blindness against which Jesus warned his opponents.

OPENING PEOPLE'S EYES

The BLIND MAN at BETHSAIDA
MARK 8:22–26

> *They came to Bethsaida, and some people brought to him a blind man whom they begged him to touch.*
>
> MARK 8:22

MARK'S GOSPEL RELATES an incident, probably typical at this stage of Jesus' ministry, when he came to the town of Bethsaida, situated on the northern tip of the Sea of Galilee. On his arrival there, the townspeople led him to a local man who was afflicted with blindness.

Reacting to their concern, Jesus took the blind man by the hand and led him out of the town, away from the crowd. There he put his saliva on the man's eyes and placed his hands on him, then asked him whether he could see anything. The blind man replied, "I can see people;

Jesus reaches out to heal the blind man in this medieval Byzantine book illumination. It was created by the monks of Mount Athos, a self-governing monastic republic situated on a peninsula in northern Greece.

they look like trees as they walk around." Jesus again placed his hands on the man's eyes, and this time the man declared himself fully cured, able to see everything clearly and sharply. Jesus then sent the recovered man home but told him not go into the town, presumably so that he would not attract undue attention.

The healing of the Bethsaida man is the only occasion recorded in the Gospels in which Jesus did not effect a full cure instantly. This account also lacks some of the typical accompaniments of Jesus' other miracles. For example, Jesus performed the healing away from the crowd; there is no mention of the necessity of faith on the part of the blind man, nor is his condition ascribed to possession by evil spirits; and it does not lead on to any teaching laden with overt symbolism – unlike, for example, the account in John's Gospel of the miracle of the man born blind (pp. 62–65), with which John links directly the idea of Jesus as the "light of the world."

+ The "blind" disciples +

Although Matthew, Luke, and John did not include this miracle in their Gospels, many scholars believe that it holds an important place in Mark's account. Just before the telling of the story, Mark alludes to the disciples' lack of perception concerning Jesus' ability to work miracles and his status as the Messiah. Jesus upbraided them for this – "Do you still not understand, still not realize? Are your minds closed? Have you eyes and do not see and do not hear? Or do you not remember [8:17, 18]?" – in terms that symbolically linked their obtuseness to the condition of the blind man of Bethsaida.

After the healing, Jesus set off with his disciples to other villages in the area around the city of Caesarea Philippi. Along the way, he asked his followers who the common people thought he was. They answered "John the Baptist," "Elijah," and "one of the prophets." These responses, like the first partial clearing of the blind man's vision, approached the true reality without fully realizing it. Like him, the disciples began dimly to perceive things – in their case, the special spiritual status of Jesus.

Then Jesus turned his attention to the disciples and asked them directly who they themselves thought he was. Peter replied that Jesus was the Christ, the Messiah, finally perceiving the full truth in the manner that the blind man had finally regained his full sight.

Also, in the same way that Jesus told the blind man not to make public what had happened, so he gave strict orders to the disciples not to disclose to anyone that he was the Christ. In this way, as some scholars argue, Mark was using the account of the miracle to embody the progressive enlightenment of the "blind" disciples. ✦

MESSAGE
—for—
TODAY

MANY PEOPLE like to see clearly where they are going in life – to have a plan and career structure, and to feel in control of their destiny. Sometimes, like the blind man, they have no vision at all of what lies just ahead. More often their perception resembles his first stage of healing – partial, imperfect. People and events that in retrospect have proved to be significant may have been only dimly perceived as such at the time.

People's difficulty in seeing where the path ahead leads provides an opportunity to place trust in God's guidance. The 19th-century British churchman John Henry Newman spoke of such trust in his hymn Lead, Kindly Light: "Keep thou my feet; I do not ask to see/The distant scene; one step enough for me."

HEALING *on the* SABBATH

The MAN *with a condition of* DROPSY

LUKE 14:1–6

❝ *And Jesus addressed the lawyers and Pharisees with the words, 'Is it against the law to cure someone on the Sabbath, or not?'* **❞**

LUKE 14:3

W HEN JESUS WAS making one of his journeys toward Jerusalem from Galilee, teaching in towns and villages as he went, an important Pharisee invited him to share a meal in his house. Neither the name of the man nor that of his town is stated in Luke's account. It was the Sabbath, according to Luke, the day of rest, and the Pharisee's guests – who included other Pharisees and lawyers – were watching Jesus closely.

There, Jesus was approached by a man who was afflicted with dropsy, a condition that causes various parts of the body to swell with excessive fluid. As if reading the unspoken thoughts of the other guests, Jesus asked aloud whether they considered it against the Jewish Law to cure someone on the Sabbath.

The Law made it clear that saving a life took precedence over other Sabbath rules; but there was much dispute about which illnesses were life-threatening, which made it a difficult question for the Pharisees to answer. If they indicated that it was contrary to the Law, they would reveal a lack of compassion. However, if they said that healing was permissible, they could undermine their position as strict upholders of the Law.

The guests, therefore, remained silent, and so gave up their right to criticize whichever course of action Jesus decided to follow. In the event, Jesus "took the man and cured him and sent him away." Perhaps Jesus felt a continuing sense of unspoken hostility and criticism from among the

Pharisees, because he questioned them again. If one of their sons (some manuscripts say "ass" instead of "son") or oxen were to fall into an open well, he demanded, would they not come to the rescue on the Sabbath? Again the guests did not feel able to answer his question.

Jesus cures the man afflicted with dropsy, at top, in this medieval English illumination. In the bottom part, Jesus talks to a tax collector named Zacchaeus, who had climbed a tree to catch a glimpse of him.

Recounted only in Luke's Gospel, the cure of the man with dropsy shows another occasion when Jesus came into conflict with his opponents over the Sabbath. Customarily, Jews took three meals on the Sabbath and often asked guests to the main midday meal, served after worship in the synagogue. It was probably this to which Jesus had been invited. It is clear from this episode that Jesus was prepared to sit at the table with people he knew to be antagonistic toward him. His refusal to reject so-called sinners and society's castoffs extended also to those who opposed him.

✝ Compassion and the Law ✝

The mealtime itself, as Luke describes it, seems to have been tense as Jesus preempted the Pharisees' criticism with his appeal for compassion. After his first question was met with silence, Jesus then turned to the suffering man. The man's affliction, dropsy, which can be caused by heart or kidney disease or by other ailments, was not uncommon at that time.

In Jewish tradition it was believed to be a punishment for sexual offenses; Herod the Great was said to have suffered from it in his feet. In any case, Jesus ignored the Pharisees' hostile scrutiny and simply cured the man.

Jesus then posed his second question. Although in theory the Law forbade an act of healing except in extreme circumstances, it did allow an animal to be removed from a life-threatening situation. Open wells, the example Jesus used, were evidently a frequent hazard in ancient Palestine. The Book of Exodus (21:33–34), for example, declares that if a man digs a well and leaves it uncovered, and an ox or donkey falls into it, then he will be liable to compensate the animal's owner.

Jesus pointed out that the Law permitted an animal to be saved on the Sabbath. How much more valuable was the health of a human. Surely the implication was clear. To this his opponents could not muster a word among them. ✦

MESSAGE
—for—
TODAY

JESUS USED the Jewish Law's teaching that the saving of life had priority over Sabbath rules to justify his healing of the man suffering from dropsy. Both by his arguments and by his actions, Jesus showed that acts of mercy are more important than religious rules.

It is easy for the legalistic aspect of religious traditions, or indeed any bureaucratic regulations, to obscure human need. Excessive red tape and obsessive attention to the letter of the law may actually subvert the good intentions behind the law itself. Wherever obeying rules stands in opposition to the exercise of compassion, it is perhaps time, as the Indian teacher and statesman Mahatma Gandhi said, "to recall the face of the poorest and weakest person you may have seen and to ask 'will he gain anything by your actions?'"

BRINGING *the* DEAD *to* LIFE

The RAISING *of* LAZARUS
JOHN 11:1–44

❝ There was a man named Lazarus of Bethany, the village of Mary and her sister, Martha, and he was ill. It was the same Mary, the sister of the sick man Lazarus, who anointed the Lord with ointment and wiped his feet with her hair. The sisters sent this message to Jesus, 'Lord, the man you love is ill.' ❞
JOHN 11:1–3

WHEN NEWS REACHED Jesus that his friend Lazarus was ill, he was on the eastern side of the Jordan River some distance from Jerusalem, where his enemies had threatened to kill him. Two days later, he declared his intention to return to Bethany, Lazarus' hometown, which lay only about 2 miles (3 km) from Jerusalem.

At first, Jesus' disciples were alarmed, reminding him that just a short time before some Jews had tried to stone him. Jesus replied: "Our friend Lazarus is at rest; I am going to wake him." The disciples, so John relates, thought that by "rest" Jesus meant "sleep." But Jesus was referring to the fact, which he apparently knew by supernatural means, that Lazarus was dead.

At Bethany, Jesus discovered that Lazarus had not only died, but had already been laid in a tomb. As soon as Martha, Lazarus' sister, heard that Jesus had arrived, she ran out to meet him and said, "Lord, if you had been here, my brother would not have died, but even now I know that God will grant whatever you ask of him." Jesus

reassured her: her brother would return from the dead, he said. Furthermore, anyone who had faith in Jesus would never die.

Martha, deeply moved, confessed her faith in him, then hurried off to tell her sister, Mary, that Jesus had come. Immediately, Mary rushed to see him, throwing herself at his feet, weeping. Jesus was greatly distressed by her tears and asked her where Lazarus had been laid to rest.

✝ Emerging from the tomb ✝

Jesus was taken to Lazarus' tomb – a cave with a large stone placed in front of it. When he ordered the stone to be removed, Martha reminded him that Lazarus had been buried for

In this fresco by the 14th-century Italian painter Giotto, Jesus blesses the figure of Lazarus as he is brought out of his cave tomb. Lazarus – looking cadaverous after his four days in the tomb – is wrapped up in a traditional linen winding cloth. A woman, at right, holds her robe up to her nose because of the noxious smell.

four days; the body would smell. To this Jesus replied, "Have I not told you that if you believe, you will see the glory of God?"

The stone was rolled away, and Jesus, looking skyward, thanked God for answering his prayer. Then he shouted, "Lazarus, come out!" As the onlookers watched the tomb's entrance, the figure of Lazarus, bound head to foot in white cloth, slowly emerged from the sepulchral darkness. Jesus said, "Unbind him, let him go free." With these words, John's account of the miracle ends.

Afterward, John goes on to say, many of the Jews who had witnessed the miracle believed in Jesus. Others, however, went to the Pharisees to inform them of Jesus' action. Fearing that Jesus might precipitate a popular uprising that the Romans would ruthlessly suppress, the Pharisees held a meeting. At this, the high priest, Caiaphas, pronounced that it would be better that "one man should die for the people, rather than that the whole nation should perish." These words of a calculating politician were also, John suggests, prophetic of the meaning of Jesus' death.

This tomb, said to be that of Lazarus at Bethany, was — like those of other wealthy Jews — cut into rock. Bodies were laid in compartments in the walls.

† For the glory of God †

The raising of Lazarus from the dead is one of the most dramatic acts Jesus performed. Although the Gospels relate that Jesus restored life to the son of the widow of Nain (pp. 30–31) and the daughter of Jairus (pp. 40–43), these acts were performed soon after the death of the people involved. Lazarus had been in the tomb for four days when Jesus raised him to life. According to Jewish belief, a dead person's spirit hovered over his or her corpse for three days before departing. In making a point of Lazarus' days in the tomb, John stressed that Lazarus was well and truly dead.

> ❝ *'Lord, by now he will smell; this is the fourth day since he died.'* ❞
>
> JOHN 11:39

The story of Lazarus has added poignancy because Lazarus and his sisters, Mary and Martha, were close personal friends of Jesus. Jesus shared the women's grief over their brother, and at one point he even broke down and wept, prompting onlookers to remark, "See how much he loved him!"

According to John, Jesus revealed the significance of Lazarus' death when he said: "This sickness will not end in death, but it is for God's glory so that through it the Son of God may be glorified." Jesus intended all along to show the glory of God through a public demonstration of his power over the dead. In this connection, Lazarus' death and coming back to life also

The aloe plant is thought to have been used in Jewish burials during New Testament times. It was crushed and mixed with myrrh and placed between the layers of cloth used to wrap the body of the deceased.

MESSAGE
—for—
TODAY

IT IS NOT SURPRISING that Martha was puzzled when Jesus said to her "I am the Resurrection and the Life." She would have thought the Resurrection was not a present person, but an event that would take place in the future. Yet John insists in his Gospel that the union of the faithful with Jesus is so close that they already share the divine life before death.

Many people of faith have drawn on divine resources to prepare for the time when death comes, either to themselves or to their loved ones. The process of bereavement may be agonizing — as it was for Lazarus' sisters. But the consolation of faith is that death is not an end but a beginning — an emergence from this world's cave of darkness to the light of the heavenly realm.

foreshadowed Jesus' own imminent fate on the cross and subsequent resurrection.

Perhaps most of all, the story of Lazarus gives a meaningful context to one of Jesus' most direct and theologically significant statements, uttered while speaking to Martha. Martha insisted that had Jesus arrived earlier, her brother would not have died in the first place. She went on to state her belief that Lazarus would be resurrected on the last day – the Day of Judgment.

While Jesus did not contradict the traditional doctrine that Martha expressed, he made it clear that eternal life is possible not after death in the distant future, but through him, in the present: "I am the Resurrection. Anyone who believes in me, even though that person dies, will live, and whoever lives and believes in me will never die." To anyone who heard this but still doubted its validity, the physical resurrection of Lazarus was the ultimate proof. ✦

An EXORCISM through PRAYER

The BOY POSSESSED by a "SPIRIT of DUMBNESS"

MARK 9:14–29; MATTHEW 17:14–21;
LUKE 9:37–43

> **❝** *They brought the boy to him, and at once the spirit of dumbness threw the boy into convulsions and he fell to the ground and lay writhing there, foaming at the mouth.* **❞**
>
> MARK 9:20

ESUS' CURE OF AN epileptic boy occurred, according to all three Synoptic Gospels, immediately after Jesus' Transfiguration. This was an event that occurred when Jesus had taken his three closest disciples, Peter, James, and John, up a mountain – possibly Mount Hermon in northern Palestine. There a radiant light had changed his appearance. At the same time, Moses and Elijah appeared beside him. These two great figures from Israel's past represented the Law and the Prophets. And God's voice spoke from the clouds, proclaiming Jesus to be his son.

After this extraordinary event, Jesus and his three companions descended from the mountain to rejoin the other disciples below. But as they approached, they saw that the disciples who had stayed behind had been surrounded by a large crowd and were now arguing with a number of scribes – the official teachers of Jewish Law.

When the people saw Jesus coming toward them, they were "struck with amazement." This was perhaps because they were not expecting him to arrive at this moment or possibly because he still bore traces of the radiant light from the Transfiguration. In any case, they ran up to him.

Jesus asked what had caused the argument. According to Mark, whose account is the most detailed of the three, a man from the crowd replied that Jesus' disciples had been unable to cure his sick son. The father described the son's affliction in terms of a spirit that threw him to the ground and made him writhe, foam at the mouth, grind his teeth, and then become rigid. In modern medical terms, the boy seems to have been suffering from a form of epilepsy.

✦ The need for faith ✦

In response, Jesus exclaimed: "Faithless generation, how much longer must I be among you? How much longer must I put up with you?" He seemed most exasperated with his disciples, whose lack of faith in him had resulted in their inability to effect an exorcism. Without further ado, he ordered the boy to be brought to him. At once, the boy fell to the ground, writhing and foaming at the mouth.

Jesus asked the father how long his son had been suffering from this condition. Since

FAITH · WHICH · WORKETH
BY · LOVE

MARK · CHAP IX · VER · 25

childhood, the father answered, then implored Jesus, if he could, to have pity on them. Jesus replied that everything was possible for one who had faith, whereupon the father cried out: "I have faith. Help my lack of faith!"

As more people gathered around him, Jesus decided it was time to act and commanded the spirit to leave the boy and never to return again. Again, the boy was thrown into fierce convulsions, until finally the evil spirit emerged from his body, shouting as it came. The boy

The father of the possessed boy implores Jesus to exorcize his son, in this detail from a 19th-century stained-glass window in Lincoln Cathedral, England. The boy was afflicted by an evil spirit that made him writhe on the ground, as he is depicted doing here.

stopped writhing and lay so still that some people thought he must be dead. But Jesus took him by the hand and helped him to stand up.

Later, when Jesus was alone with his disciples, they asked him why they had been unable to perform the exorcism. According to Mark, Jesus said that the spirit was of a type that could be driven out only by prayer.

✝ Moses, Jesus, and faith ✝

The healing of the epileptic boy provides a stark contrast with the scene of the Transfiguration that immediately precedes it. While on the mountain, Jesus' face had "shone like the sun" and he had communed with two of the greatest figures from Israel's past. Down below on the plain, however, he was plunged back into the realm of ordinary mortals beset by evil spirits, disease, and doubt.

The disciples' failure to perform the exorcism underlined the enormity of Jesus' task to bring about God's kingdom on Earth, eliciting from him a blast against this "faithless generation" that echoes the complaint made by God to Moses in the Old Testament Book of Numbers about the Israelites' lack of trust: "How much longer will they refuse to trust me, in spite of all the signs I have displayed among them [14:11]?"

> ❝ At once the father of the boy cried out, 'I have faith. Help my lack of faith!' And when Jesus saw that a crowd was gathering, he rebuked the unclean spirit. 'Deaf and dumb spirit... come out of him...' ❞
>
> MARK 9:24, 25

Some biblical commentators have pointed out parallels between Moses and Jesus in this episode. In the same way, for example, that Moses went up Mount Sinai for his meeting with God and to receive the Law, so Jesus went up a mountain and encountered the divine. And, just as Moses returned from the mountain to witness feuding

Mount Hermon in northern Palestine was probably the site of Jesus' Transfiguration, immediately after which he cured the possessed boy. The mountain is in fact a range, 18 miles (29 km) long, whose highest peak rises 9,232 feet (2,814 m).

among the Israelites, so Jesus, on his arrival on the plain, was greeted with the arguments between his disciples and the scribes.

The central issue in both stories is faith. In the Gospel account, the disciples' lack of faith prevented them from healing the boy. When the father begged Jesus to save his son, Jesus responded with one of the cardinal truths of Christianity: "Everything is possible for one who has faith." The father's reaction – that he had some faith but needed Jesus' help to reinforce it – has struck a chord with Christians ever since.

The father of the afflicted son approached Jesus with a spirit of humility that may be

implicitly contrasted to that of the disciples. Earlier in his ministry, Jesus had given them the ability to perform exorcisms: "So they came to him and he appointed twelve; they were to be his companions and to be sent out to proclaim the message with the power to drive out devils [Mark 3:13-15]." Now, they were genuinely puzzled by their lack of potency in healing.

Mark relates that Jesus stressed the need for prayer, implying that only through submission to God would a person be able to drive out an evil spirit, such as the one they had just encountered. In Matthew's Gospel, by contrast, Jesus told the disciples that their failure was a result of a lack of faith, and spelled out in no uncertain terms what even the smallest faith could achieve: "In truth I tell you, if your faith is the size of a mustard seed, you will say to this mountain, 'Move from here to there,' and it will move; nothing will be impossible for you." ✦

MESSAGE
—for—
TODAY

FAITH — or the need for faith — lies at the heart of this miracle. Many people identify with the plea of the epileptic boy's father: "Help my lack of faith!" He saw clearly that his and the disciples' lack of faith had made the healing of his son impossible.

The Jewish philosopher Martin Buber, reflecting on the Holocaust, spoke of "moments of faith." He said that there are times when "the smoke of the burning children blots out faith" and other moments when the vision of the redeemer is clear. Daily news headlines proclaiming disaster and violence can make it easy to despair about the prospect of peace and justice. But faith in God can help people strengthen their hope that love and goodness are stronger than hatred and evil. In the exercise of such faith, people have often participated in God's work of redemption.

A GRATEFUL SAMARITAN

The TEN VICTIMS of SKIN DISEASE
LUKE 17:11–19

> " *They stood some way off and called to him,*
> *'Jesus! Master! Take pity on us.'* "
> LUKE 17:12–13

MAKING HIS WAY toward Jerusalem via the border of Samaria and Galilee, Jesus came to one of the villages in the area. As he approached its outskirts, he was greeted by the sight of ten men suffering from a skin disease, probably leprosy. Because, according to the Jewish Law, they were ritually unclean, they stood some distance away from Jesus and beseeched him to take pity on them.

Jesus' response was to tell them to go and show themselves "to the priests" – which was the procedure the Law required to confirm that a cure had been successful. As they walked off toward the priests at Jesus' command, they discovered that they had been healed, and one of them, a man from Samaria, turned back, cried out praises to God, and threw himself at Jesus' feet, thanking him for his cure. The Samaritan's spontaneous gratitude prompted Jesus to remark: "Were not all ten made clean? The other nine, where are they? It seems that no one has come back to give praise to God, except this foreigner."

Jesus commands the ten lepers to confirm their cure with the priests, in this 11th-century German illumination. The cured Samaritan leper thanks Jesus, at right.

He then turned to the man and said: "Stand up and go on your way. Your faith has saved you."

This miracle took place during the last phase of Jesus' life, as he was making his final journey to Jerusalem. In his account, Luke does not mention the name of the village where the healing took place. But wherever it was, Jesus' fame as a healer had evidently reached it, since the men already knew his name and addressed him as "Master." Unlike his healing of the single leper (pp. 20–21), reported in all the Synoptic Gospels, Jesus did not actually touch these sufferers but simply told them to report to the priests, implying that their cures had been effected.

✝ A despised people ✝

The focus of the story centers on the reaction of these men. Only one shows explicit gratitude for the miracle, and he is not a Jew, but a Samaritan. This is where the surprise of the story lies. Racially, the Samaritans were descendants of Jews who had escaped deportation by the Assyrians – who had conquered the kingdom of Israel in 721 BC – and various other peoples the latter had introduced into the region. Over a period of time, hostility developed between the Samaritans and the Jews, continuing into New Testament times.

Earlier in his Gospel, Luke had addressed Jewish prejudice against the people of Samaria with the parable of the good Samaritan (10:29–37), who cared for a man who had been attacked by robbers. Now, in his account of the miracle of the men with skin disease, he drives home the point that Jesus' compassion extended to both Jews and Samaritans, and that the latter could be as capable of piety and joyous gratitude as the children of Israel, God's chosen people.

In Jesus' final words to the Samaritan – "Your faith has saved you" – he suggests that the man has been not only physically but also spiritually cleansed, unlike his fellow sufferers, his eyes opened to a new way of life exemplified by Jesus. ✦

MESSAGE
— for —
TODAY

RECOVERY AFTER a long illness can involve spiritual as well as physical healing. A time in the hospital may increase awareness of the sufferings of others; and just as the Jewish and Samaritan victims of skin disease had learned to live together, so lying in a bed next to a person of another race or color may dispel prejudice.

After recovery, however, people may soon forget the efforts of those who worked long hours or had the technical expertise or compassion to help them. Yet gratitude is important, not simply as a way of recognizing the efforts of others, but also as an expression of joy, which in turn can accelerate convalescence. As the Book of Proverbs says: "A glad heart is excellent medicine, a depressed spirit wastes the bones away [17:22]."

A REWARD *for* PERSISTENCE

The BLIND MAN *of* JERICHO

MARK 10:46–52; MATTHEW 20:29–34; LUKE 18:35–43

> *When he heard that it was Jesus of Nazareth, he began to shout and cry out, 'Son of David, Jesus, have pity on me.'*
>
> MARK 10:47

THE LAST HEALING that Jesus performed before his triumphal entry into Jerusalem and his trial and death on the cross – according to the three Synoptic Gospels – occurred at Jericho, about 15 miles (25 km) northeast of Jerusalem. Accompanied by his disciples and a large crowd of pilgrims, Jesus was making his final, fateful journey to the Jewish capital to celebrate the Passover festival. According to the account in

Mark's Gospel, a blind beggar named Bartimaeus was sitting by the side of the road as Jesus was leaving Jericho. When he heard that Jesus was walking past, he began to cry out his name, addressing him as the "Son of David" – a title associated with the Messiah.

***On the outskirts** of Jericho, Jesus cures Bartimaeus, the blind man, in this painting by the French artist Nicolas Poussin (1594–1665).*

In Luke's Gospel, the beggar is not named, and Matthew states that there were two beggars, not one. However, the three accounts are so similar that it seems likely that it is the same incident.

Mark records that as the beggar cried out to Jesus for pity, some of the crowd told him to be quiet – prompting Bartimaeus to shout louder. Jesus evidently heard the supplicant, because he stopped and ordered the beggar to be brought to him. So Bartimaeus walked over to Jesus and asked Jesus to restore his sight. Jesus replied that his faith had saved him, and immediately the man's vision returned. He then followed Jesus along the road and, in Luke, began to praise God.

✝ Son of David ✝

The cure of the blind man, or men, of Jericho comes at the end of Jesus' healing ministry and heralds the beginning of the end of his life on Earth. The miracle not only stands at a pivotal point in the Gospel narrative. It also contains the first public recognition of Jesus' messiahship. Until this incident, only people possessed by evil spirits and the disciples had acknowledged Jesus as the Messiah, and he had told them to be silent on the subject. Now, when the beggar addressed him as "Son of David," Jesus did not order him to be quiet.

Some scholars also see the story as the classic model of Christian discipleship. As Jesus walked past the beggar, the man saw that his one hope of salvation lay at hand. Then, despite being rebuked by the crowd, he continued to shout out to Jesus. When he was finally told that Jesus would speak to him, he seized his chance; his insight that Jesus was the Messiah was rewarded by physical sight.

Finally, instead of melting back into the crowd to celebrate his newfound vision, the beggar followed in the footsteps of Jesus, praising God as he went. The basic elements and rewards of Christian discipleship are thus encapsulated: recognition of Jesus, faith, perseverance, salvation, and following the path of Christ. ◆

MESSAGE
—for—
TODAY

BY THE TIME OF this miracle, Jesus' disciples realized that they were traveling in the company of greatness. Mark says that on the road to Jericho, the disciples James and John asked Jesus to guarantee their privileged status in the kingdom of Heaven. Jesus reminded them that whoever would be great must act as a servant, as he himself had come to serve humankind. Again and again, he demonstrated this attitude. He put it into practice by healing Bartimaeus, ignoring those who had found him unworthy of attention.

For his part, Bartimaeus did not let his lowly status deter him from his efforts to be cured by Jesus. Even in the exercise of faith, people must sometimes overcome feelings of low self-esteem, ignore discouraging voices, and show the sort of single-mindedness that Bartimaeus displayed.

A SYMBOL of UNFRUITFULNESS

The BARREN FIG TREE

MARK 11:12–14, 20–24; MATTHEW 21:18–22

" Seeing a fig tree by the road, he went up to it and found nothing on it but leaves. "

MATTHEW 21:19

THE DAY AFTER his triumphal entry into Jerusalem, Jesus performed arguably his most puzzling miracle. He cursed a fig tree outside the city walls, the only instance recorded in the Gospels in which Jesus performed a "punitive" miracle.

According to Mark, Jesus was leaving the village of Bethany, situated about 2 miles (3 km) from Jerusalem, to return to the city. Feeling hungry, he walked over to a fig tree that was in leaf, but then saw that, despite its lush foliage, the tree bore no fruit. So he cursed it with the words, "May no one ever eat fruit from you again."

After this, Mark relates, Jesus entered Jerusalem and went to the Temple, where he ousted those who were using the place for commercial transactions. The following morning, Jesus and his disciples again passed the fig tree and saw that it had "withered to the roots." When Peter remarked that Jesus' curse had taken effect, Jesus responded by instructing his followers about the power of faith and prayer.

Jesus cursed the fig tree because although its leaves had sprouted and covered the branches with dense foliage, it had not produced any fruit.

In Matthew, the incident is not interruped by the Temple episode and, after Jesus' curse, the tree withered instantly. When the disciples expressed their amazement, Jesus answered them also with words about faith and prayer.

✝ The symbolic tree ✝

Jesus' cursing of the tree presents various problems, not least that it appears to be an act of destruction against a non-sentient part of creation at variance with the love and compassion that otherwise characterized his behavior. Mark points out that it was not the season for the tree to produce fruit, which makes Jesus' action seem even more unreasonable.

Some scholars think that Mark and Matthew included the incident because of the teaching on faith that follows it. But the miracle seems to exemplify judgment, not faith or prayer. As such, many scholars interpret the story symbolically, seeing in it an image of Israel's attitude to Jesus. In the same way that the tree had leaves but no fruit, so the Jewish nation, the Gospel writers may be suggesting, had outward religious ceremonies; but when Jesus sought spiritual fruit beneath the external show, he found nothing.

The image of the tree appears, too, in a parable that is recounted by Luke (13:6–9). In Luke's story, the tree seems to represent the Jews' response to the coming of God's kingdom as ushered in by Jesus. It apparently counsels patience and the granting of one last chance for a change of attitude to occur.

Many scholars infer from this that the cursing of the fig tree was originally a parable, with imagery similar to that found in Luke's story. Over a period of time, the oral accounts of the parable may have become confused. In this case, the significance of the story would lie in the gravity of Jesus' attitude toward Israel and that, as he drew closer to his death, he seems to have finally discounted the Jews' willingness to respond to his teaching and ministry. ✦

MESSAGE
—for—
TODAY

AT HIS TRIAL, Jesus was accused of threatening to destroy the Temple in Jerusalem. In AD 70, at about the time when the Gospels were first being written down, the Temple and the city were actually destroyed by the Romans. Some contemporary Christians thought this had been prefigured by the story of the fig tree.

The tree had beautiful leaves, but no fruit. Equally, however glorious the architecture of a religious building like the Temple, or indeed the dress and ritual of any religious ceremony, it is barren unless it encourages faith and good works in the people who attend it. As Jesus insisted, people will ultimately be judged not on any outward show of piety, but on what proceeds from the depth of their being.

LOVE *your* ENEMIES

HEALING *the* EAR *of the* HIGH PRIEST'S SERVANT

LUKE 22:47–51

❝ *And one of them struck the high priest's servant*
and cut off his right ear. **❞**
LUKE 22:50

J ESUS' LAST MIRACLE before his death on the cross occurred at the moment of his arrest in the garden of Gethsemane. Only Luke tells of the healing, but the other Gospel writers recount the events up to and after the miracle.

Following the Last Supper, at which Jesus shared bread and wine with his disciples, they all went to the Mount of Olives just outside the walls of Jerusalem. There, within what John describes as a garden and Mark refers to as "a plot of land

called Gethsemane [14:32]," Jesus and Peter, John, and James (according to Mark and Matthew) withdrew from the other disciples.

Jesus sensed the imminent agony of the crucifixion and prayed to God in his greatest expression of anguish. His disciples were unable to stay awake with him, and as he chided them for

A follower of Jesus, at left, cuts off the ear of the high priest's servant as Jesus is shown being kissed by Judas, in this medieval Italian painting.

falling asleep, a crowd sent to arrest him by the Jewish authorities appeared. They were led by Judas, one of Jesus' 12 disciples.

† Resisting aggression †

After Judas had identified Jesus by giving him a kiss – described as the most ironical kiss in history – Mark recounts that one of the bystanders then drew his sword and cut off the ear of the high priest's servant. Matthew and Luke say that it was one of Jesus' followers who committed the deed, while John actually names the aggressor as Peter and the victim as Malchus.

According to Luke, Jesus put an end to the violence with the words "That is enough," and touched the man's ear and healed him. Then he denounced those who had come to capture him, pointing out that, contrary to what their show of arms might suggest, he was not a bandit. In fact, he said, they could have arrested him at any time during his visits to the Temple. The crowd then seized Jesus and took him to the high priest's house, where he was tried.

The healing of the servant's ear is significant because it shows that even in his darkest hour, Jesus maintained his compassion and healing powers in the cause of others. Once and for all, it showed his enemies – who had been prepared for armed resistance – that he was no brigand or political firebrand, but a peaceable Messiah who eschewed violence and healed the sick and injured.

At the same time, Jesus showed his disciples by personal example the way they should react toward an aggressive force. In his Sermon on the Mount (Matthew 5–7), Jesus had stated that if a person was slapped on the right cheek, he or she should turn and offer the left one. Here, according to Matthew, he told his spirited follower: "Put your sword back, for all who draw the sword will die by the sword [26:52]." In Luke, he reinforced his teaching by healing an enemy – and this in spite of the shadow of the cross lengthening toward him. ✦

MESSAGE
—for—
TODAY

IN THE GARDEN of Gethsemane, Jesus accepted his fate without reprisal; but one of his followers – John says it was Peter – had to be commanded to put away his sword. Throughout the days that followed, when Jesus was tried, tortured, and put to death, he continued to reject violence, but he went on caring for others.

Throughout history, Christians have sometimes resorted to the sword in the cause of their faith. Today, some are tempted to use modern weapons such as aggressive advertising or exploitive fundraising to promote their aims. But it is loving care, as shown by Mother Teresa's ministry to the dying in India or the courage of the South African Archbishop Desmond Tutu in his opposition to apartheid, that is the most Christlike advertisement for the faith.

An ENCOUNTER with the RISEN CHRIST

The MIRACULOUS HAUL of FISH

JOHN 21:1–14

" Jesus called out, 'Haven't you caught anything,
friends?' And when they answered,
'No,' he said, 'Throw the net out to starboard
and you'll find something.' "

JOHN 21:5–6

FTER HIS CRUCIFIXION, and resurrection from the dead, Jesus is reported to have appeared to his disciples on more than one occasion. In John's Gospel, the last time this occurred was at the Sea of Galilee. Seven of the disciples had gone fishing on the lake, and although they had cast their nets throughout the night, they had failed to catch anything.

Then, as dawn broke, they heard a voice ring out across the water from a person – whom they did not recognize as Jesus – standing on the shore. Jesus asked them if they had caught any fish and, on hearing that they had been unsuccessful, told them to throw the net from the right side of the boat. The disciples carried out what he commanded and promptly caught so many fish that they were unable to haul the net in.

One of the disciples – his name is not given, but he is described by John as the one "whom Jesus loved" – said to Peter, referring to the figure by the edge of the lake, "It is the Lord." At once, Peter sprang into action. Tying his outer garment over his loincloth, he jumped into the water and made his way toward the shore, followed by the other disciples in the boat.

On reaching dry land, they found that a charcoal fire had been lit, with fish cooking on top and bread laid beside it. Jesus was standing nearby and told them to bring some of the fish they had just caught. When the net was dragged to the land, it was found that, although it was full of 153 large fish, it had remained unbroken.

Jesus invited the disciples to join him in eating breakfast, and by this time they all knew his identity. Jesus then broke the bread and distributed it along with the fish. John ends the account of the miracle with the statement that it was "the third time that Jesus revealed himself to the disciples after rising from the dead."

† Luke's haul of fish †

John's account of the haul of 153 fish has a number of similarities with that of the miraculous haul of fish recounted by Luke (5:1–14), in which Jesus called Peter to be his disciple. In that story, Jesus was standing by the Sea of Galilee when, to avoid being crushed by the gathered crowd, he got into a fisherman's boat – which turned out to be Peter's – and began to teach from it. When he had finished, he told

Peter to take his boat out into deeper water and let down his nets. Peter replied that he had been fishing all night in vain, but nevertheless complied with Jesus' command. This time, however, he was successful: he caught so many fish that the nets broke and he had to call out to his companions in another boat to help him. Even so, the number of fish was such that "they filled both boats to sinking point."

Amazed at the miracle and struck by Jesus' power, Peter then fell at the Lord's knees and said: "Leave me, Lord; I am a sinful man." However, Jesus told Peter not to be afraid and said that from now on he would be "catching" people.

As his companions haul up a net full of fish after a fruitless night at sea, Peter walks toward Jesus, who waits for him on the shore, in this medieval Italian painting.

The most striking similarity between John's and Luke's stories – apart from the miraculous haul – is that they both focus on Peter, Jesus' foremost disciple. There is also a circular aspect to the two accounts. In the same way that Peter first met Jesus through his occupation as a fisherman, so too, John relates, he saw Jesus for the last time in a fishing context. According to Luke, Jesus informed Peter that he would become a fisher of people. And in John, after Jesus had questioned

Peter three times about his love for him and had prophesied his martyrdom, he then said "Follow me," again confirming his discipleship.

❝ Simon Peter went aboard and dragged the net ashore, full of big fish, one hundred and fifty-three of them . . . ❞

JOHN 21:11

Given this link, some scholars have suggested that the two stories might derive from one historical event. But, despite the similarities, the setting and atmosphere are different. In Luke, Jesus was standing among crowds about to start his Galilean ministry and wanting to recruit companions to help him spread the word of God. In John, where the scene is firmly established after Jesus' death, he appeared as a lone figure on the shore; the tone is low key, with the disciples returning to their secular occupations after their extraordinarily eventful association with Jesus during his lifetime, and there is a sense of anticlimax.

✝ The races of the world ✝

The two hauls of fish also differ. In Luke, it is said that the weight of the fish broke the nets. John is more precise, stating that the number of fish was 153. This specific number has puzzled commentators from the earliest times. Saint Cyril of Alexandria (*d.* 444) thought, for reasons that are not entirely clear, that the number represented three elements: 100 stood for the Gentile world;

Jewish fishermen still ply their trade on the Sea of Galilee – just as Jesus' disciples did some 2,000 years ago.

This early Christian epitaph depicts two fish, which are a symbol of Christianity. This is because the Greek word for fish, ichthus, *is an acrostic for* Iesous Christos Theou Uios Soter – *Jesus Christ, God's Son, Savior.*

50 for the Jews; and 3 for the Trinity. But the interpretation that many modern scholars favor is based on a tradition, current in antiquity, that the number of species of fish was 153. The haul of fish would then represent all the races of the world, embodying the idea that the missionary endeavor of the church is truly universal. And the fact that the net was not broken implies that the church would be capable of containing all nations.

Finally, in John, Jesus shared breakfast with the disciples – a meal of fish and bread that recalls the food in the feeding of the 5,000 (pp. 48–51), which itself foreshadowed the Last Supper and its commemoration in the Eucharist, or Mass. Indeed, in some early Christian representations of the eucharistic meal, it is not bread and wine that is depicted but bread and fish.

It is as if John is stressing that the sacramental meal of the Last Supper was not a one-time event: the risen Christ will provide spiritual sustenance wherever the faithful may gather, and through them he will welcome into the Christian fellowship all the peoples of the world. ✦

MESSAGE —for— TODAY

AFTER AN UPLIFTING spiritual or emotional experience, people may find that their lives can never be the same again. They may, like Peter and his companions, try to go back to their old, familiar way of living, but now find it as empty as the disciples' fishing nets.

Once a person has given a commitment to working for God's kingdom, it is difficult, despite the temptations, to return to a more secure, perhaps more lucrative, livelihood. But those who pursue their vision may find that the sense of fulfillment they enjoy more than compensates for poor working conditions or a low salary. Furthermore, it is only through pursuing the right path, no matter what the cost, that people gain ultimate meaning in their lives, just as Peter did only when he chose to follow the risen Jesus.

MICROPEDIA of MIRACLES

THE MIRACLES THAT the Gospel writers treated as particularly significant have already been related and discussed in this book. Other miracles are outlined here in approximate chronological order.

The TWO BLIND MEN
MATTHEW 9:27–31

As Jesus was ministering and healing around the town of Capernaum, two blind men confronted and followed him, shouting for pity. Eventually, Jesus asked them if they truly believed in his power. When they professed their faith in God, Jesus touched their eyes saying, "According to your faith, let it be done to you." Immediately, the men's sight was restored. Jesus commanded them to remain silent about the cure, but they were unable to suppress their desire to spread the news.

The DUMB POSSESSED MAN
MATTHEW 9:32–34

Immediately after Jesus had healed the two blind men in Capernaum, a possessed man who was unable to speak was brought to him. Jesus drove the evil spirit out of him so that he was able to utter words. The miracle amazed the gathered crowd, with the exception of the Pharisees, who argued that only someone in league with the devil could overpower an evil spirit.

The MAN with a WITHERED HAND
MATTHEW 12:9–14; MARK 3:1–6; LUKE 6:6–11

At some point during his ministry in Galilee, Jesus attended a synagogue where he met a man who had a withered hand. Because this meeting took place on the Sabbath, the day of rest, the Pharisees saw their chance to trap Jesus into breaking the Sabbath law, which prohibited healing as work. According to Matthew, they asked Jesus if it were permitted to cure on the Sabbath. Mark records that his reply – "Is it permitted on the Sabbath day to do good, or to do evil; to save life, or to kill?"– reduced them to silence. Mark also says that Jesus was angered by their attitude and commanded the man to hold out his hand, which Jesus restored.

The BLIND and MUTE POSSESSED MAN
MATTHEW 12:22–32

After curing the man with the withered hand, Jesus "withdrew from the district" and arrived at another town. A possessed man who was blind and unable to speak was brought to him, and Jesus cured the man before an astonished crowd. The Pharisees were among the onlookers and saw the miracle as proof that Jesus was working with the the devil. Jesus perceived their thoughts and told them that his power came from the Spirit of God. To stress the gravity of his opponents' perverted accusation, Jesus said, "Anyone who says a word against the Son of man will be forgiven; but no one who speaks against the Holy Spirit will be forgiven either in this world or in the next."

The ROYAL OFFICIAL'S SON
JOHN 4:46–54

On one occasion while he was in Galilee, Jesus went to the town of Cana. There he met a royal official whose son was dying in Capernaum, about 20 miles (30 km) away. The official asked Jesus to save the child, but Jesus questioned his faith, suggesting that it rested on the need actually to witness a successful miracle. When the man persisted, however, Jesus sent him home, telling him that his son was cured. On the way the official met his servants, who told him that the boy had revived at the time Jesus had said, "Your son will live." John refers to this miracle as the "second sign," the first being the wedding at Cana (pp. 10–13).

The FEEDING of the FOUR THOUSAND

MATTHEW 15:32–39; MARK 8:1–10

At one point in his ministry, Jesus left Galilee and went to the Gentile district of Decapolis, which lay mostly east of the Jordan River. A crowd of about 4,000 followed him for three days. Jesus was concerned for the crowd, who had to travel a long way to get back home and had nothing to eat. He asked the disciples if they had supplies, but they could produce only seven loaves and a few fish. Jesus told the crowd to sit down. He gave thanks, broke the bread, and blessed the fish. He then asked the disciples to distribute the food. There was such an abundance that after everyone had eaten, seven baskets of scraps remained.

Although most scholars regard the feeding of the 4,000 as a different version of the feeding of the 5,000 (pp. 48–51), it is presented as a separate miracle in the Gospels.

The CRIPPLED WOMAN

LUKE 13:10–17

One Sabbath, during his journey from Galilee to Jerusalem, Jesus entered a synagogue, where he met a woman who had been crippled and bent over for 18 years. He declared that the woman was cured, then laid his hands on her. She immediately straightened up.

The president of the synagogue was indignant that Jesus had broken the Sabbath by working. Jesus stressed to all present the importance of compassion over the Law. He reminded them that they cared for their animals by untying them and giving them water on the Sabbath; so how could compassion for a suffering woman be wrong? After listening to Jesus, his opponents were left, "covered with confusion."

Jesus heals the crippled woman, in this detail from an 11th-century German manuscript.

IMPOSVIT IHC MANVS MVLIERI QVAE ERAT INCLINATA, ET CONFESTIM ERECTA EST.

BIBLIOGRAPHY

Argyle, A.W. *The Gospel According to Matthew.* Cambridge University Press, Cambridge, 1963

Ashe, Geoffrey *Miracles.* Routledge and Kegan Paul, London, 1978

Barclay, William *And He Had Compassion.* St. Andrews Press, Edinburgh, 1970
– *Gospel of Matthew.* St. Andrews Press, Edinburgh, 1975
– *Gospel of Mark.* St. Andrews Press, Edinburgh, 1975
– *Gospel of Luke.* St. Andrews Press, Edinburgh, 1975
– *Gospel of John.* St. Andrews Press, Edinburgh, 1975

Barrett, C.K. *The Gospel According to St. John.* SPCK, London, 1962

Braybrooke, Marcus *Time to Meet.* SCM Press, London, 1990

Brown, Colin *Miracles and the Critical Mind.* Eerdmans, Grand Rapids, 1984

Brown, Raymond E. *The Community of the Beloved Disciple.* Paulist Press, New York, 1979

Caird, G.B. *St. Luke.* Penguin, London, 1963

Callister, Frank *One World Not Two: An Examination of the Bible Wonders in the Old Testament and the New Testament.* Religious Education Press, Oxford, 1968

Evans, C.F. *St. Luke.* SCM Press Ltd., London, 1990

Farmer, H.H. *The World and God: A Study of Prayer, Providence and Miracle in the Christian Tradition.* James Nisbet and Co., London, 1936

Fenton, J.C. *Saint Matthew.* Penguin, London, 1963
– *The Gospel According to John.* Clarendon Press, Oxford, 1970

Fuller, R.H. *Interpreting the Miracles.* SCM Press Ltd., London, 1936

Geisler, Norman L. *Miracles and Modern Thought.* Zondervan, Grand Rapids, 1982

Kee, Howard Clark *Medicine, Miracle and Magic in the New Testament Times.* Cambridge University Press, Cambridge, 1986

Keller, Ernst *Miracles in Dispute: A Continuing Debate.* SCM Press Ltd., London, 1969

Lewis, C.S. *Miracles.* Geoffrey Bles, London, 1947

Lightfoot, R.H. *St. John's Gospel.* Oxford University Press, Oxford, 1956

Loos Van Der, Dr. H. *The Miracles of Jesus.* E.J. Brill, Leiden, 1965

Marsh, John *Saint John.* Penguin, London, 1968

Melinsky, M.A.H. *Healing Miracles: An Examination from History.* A.R. Mowbray, London, 1965

Moule, C.F.D. *Miracles.* A.R. Mowbray, London, 1965

Nineham, D.E. *Saint Mark.* Penguin, London, 1963

Rawlinson, E.J. *The Gospel According to St. Mark.* Methuen, London, 1925

Richards, Hubert John *The Miracles of Jesus: What Really Happened.* Collins, London, 1975

Richardson, Alan *The Miracle Stories of the Gospels.* SCM Press Ltd., London, 1941

Swinburne, Richard *The Concept of Miracle.* Macmillan, London, 1970
– *(ed.) Miracles.* Collier Macmillan, London, 1989

Taylor, Vincent *The Gospel According to St. Mark.* Macmillan, London, 1963

Temple, William *Readings in St. John's Gospel.* Macmillan, London, 1961

Theisen, Gerd *The Miracle Stories of the Early Christian Tradition.* T & T Clark, Edinburgh, 1983

Williams, T.C. *The Idea of the Miraculous.* Macmillan, Basingstoke, 1990

INDEX

ACKNOWLEDGMENTS

ILLUSTRATIONS

David Atkinson (map) **9**; Debbie Hinks (illustration symbols).

PICTURE CREDITS

t = top, **b** = bottom

1 Sonia Halliday Photographs; **2** Robert Harding Picture Library; **3** Sonia Halliday Photographs; **5** British Museum/Bridgeman Art Library; **6** Victoria & Albert Museum/Bridgeman Art Library; **11** AKG, London; **12** Fred Mayer/Magnum; **13** Ancient Art & Architecture Collection; **15** Museum Catharijneconvent/Ruben de Heer; **16** Zefa Picture Library; **18** Agnew & Sons/Bridgeman Art Library; **20** Athens National Library/Erich Lessing/AKG, London; **22–23** Sonia Halliday Photographs; **24** Ancient Art & Architecture Collection; **27** Sonia Halliday Photographs; **28** Fred Mayer/Magnum; **29** Zefa Picture Library; **30** AKG, London; **33** York City Art Gallery/Bridgeman Art Library; **34** Sonia Halliday Photographs; **35** Bodleian Library; **37** Hessisches Landesmuseum, Darmstadt/Bridgeman Art Library; **38** Jane Taylor/Sonia Halliday Photographs; **39** Sonia Halliday Photographs; **41** Musee Lapidaire, Arles/Erich Lessing/AKG, London; **42t** Sonia Halliday Photographs, **42b** Museum of London; **44** Zefa Picture Library; **45** Courtesy of the Trustees, The National Gallery, London; **46** Jane Taylor/Sonia Halliday Photographs; **49** Sonia Halliday Photographs; **50** David Young/Colorific!; **51** Fotomas Index; **53** Kunsthalle, Hamburg/AKG, London; **54** Sonia Halliday Photographs; **55** Sistine Chapel, Vatican/AKG, London; **57** Sonia Halliday Photographs; **58** Ancient Art & Architecture Collection; **59** Erich Lessing/AKG, London; **60–63** Sonia Halliday Photographs; **64t** Zefa Picture Library, **64b** Erich Lessing/AKG, London; **66** National Library, Athens/AKG, London; **68** Master and Fellows of Corpus Christi College, Cambridge; **71** Bridgeman Art Library; **72** Erich Lessing/AKG, London; **73** Nigel J. Dennis/NHPA; **75–77** Sonia Halliday Photographs; **78** Germanisches Nationalmuseum; **80** Erich Lessing/AKG, London; **82** Stephen Dalton/NHPA; **84–7** Museo dell'Opera del Duomo, Siena/Bridgeman Art Library; **88** Sonia Halliday Photographs; **91** Escorial/AKG, London; **96** Sonia Halliday Photographs.

If the publishers have unwittingly infringed copyright in any of the illustrations reproduced, they would pay an appropriate fee on being satisfied of the owner's title.

Jesus presides at the wedding feast at Cana, in this detail from a 13th-century stained glass window from Canterbury Cathedral in England.